Philosophy and Childhood

Other Palgrave Pivot titles

Tom Watson (editor): Eastern European Perspectives on the Development of Public Relations: Other Voices

Erik Paul: Australia as US Client State: The Geopolitics of De-Democratization and Insecurity

Floyd Weatherspoon: African-American Males and the U.S. Justice System of Marginalization: A National Tragedy

Mark Axelrod: No Symbols Where None Intended: Literary Essays from Laclos to Beckett

Paul M. W. Hackett: Facet Theory and the Mapping Sentence: Evolving Philosophy, Use and Application

Irwin Wall: France Votes: The Election of François Hollande

David J. Staley: Brain, Mind and Internet: A Deep History and Future

Georgiy Voloshin: The European Union's Normative Power in Central Asia: Promoting Values and Defending Interests

Shane McCorristine: William Corder and the Red Barn Murder: Journeys of the Criminal Body

Catherine Blair: Securing Pension Provision: The Challenge of Reforming the Age of Entitlement

Zarlasht M. Razeq: UNDP's Engagement with the Private Sector, 1994–2011

James Martin: Drugs on the Dark Net: How Cryptomarkets Are Transforming the Global Trade in Illicit Drugs

Shin Yamashiro: American Sea Literature: Seascapes, Beach Narratives, and Underwater Explorations

Sudershan Goel, Barbara A. Sims, and Ravi Sodhi: Domestic Violence Laws in the United States and India: A Systematic Comparison of Backgrounds and Implications

Gregory Sandstrom: Human Extension: An Alternative to Evolutionism, Creationism and Intelligent Design

Kirsten Harley and Gary Wickham: Australian Sociology: Fragility, Survival, Rivalry

Eugene Halton: From the Axial Age to the Moral Revolution: John Stuart-Glennie, Karl Jaspers, and a New Understanding of the Idea

Joseph Kupfer: Meta-Narrative in the Movies: Tell Me a Story

Sami Pihlström: Taking Evil Seriously

Ben La Farge: The Logic of Wish and Fear: New Perspectives on Genres of Western Fiction

Samuel Taylor-Alexander: On Face Transplantation: Life and Ethics in Experimental Biomedicine

Graham Oppy: Reinventing Philosophy of Religion: An Opinionated Introduction

Ian I. Mitroff and Can M. Alpaslan: The Crisis-Prone Society: A Brief Guide to Managing the Beliefs That Drive Risk in Business

Takis S. Pappas: Populism and Crisis Politics in Greece

G. Douglas Atkins: T.S. Eliot and the Fulfillment of Christian Poetics palgrave▶pivot

Philosophy and Childhood: Critical Perspectives and Affirmative Practices

Walter Omar Kohan

Professor of Philosophy of Education, State University of Rio de Janeiro, Brazil

palgrave
macmillan

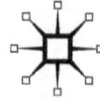

PHILOSOPHY AND CHILDHOOD
Copyright © Walter Omar Kohan, 2014.
Foreword © Maughn Gregory, 2014.

All rights reserved.

First published in 2014 by
PALGRAVE MACMILLAN®
in the United States—a division of St. Martin's Press LLC,
175 Fifth Avenue, New York, NY 10010.

Where this book is distributed in the UK, Europe and the rest of the world, this is by Palgrave Macmillan, a division of Macmillan Publishers Limited, registered in England, company number 785998, of Houndmills, Basingstoke, Hampshire RG21 6XS.

Palgrave Macmillan is the global academic imprint of the above companies and has companies and representatives throughout the world.

Palgrave® and Macmillan® are registered trademarks in the United States, the United Kingdom, Europe and other countries.

ISBN: 978-1-13746-9-182 EPUB
ISBN: 978-1-13746-9-175 PDF
ISBN: 978-1-13746-9-168 Hardback

Library of Congress Cataloging-in-Publication Data is available from the Library of Congress.

A catalogue record of the book is available from the British Library.

First edition: 2014

www.palgrave.com/pivot

DOI: 10.1057/9781137469175

*To Valeska, Giulietta and Milena,
My deepest childhood*

Contents

Foreword viii
Maughn Gregory

Preface and Acknowledgments xi

Part I Philosophy for Children: Critical Perspectives

1 Some Biographical Remarks and Philosophical Questions within Philosophy for Children 2

2 Celebrating Thirty Years of Philosophy for Children 11

3 Good-Bye to Matthew Lipman (and Ann Margaret Sharp) 21

4 The Politics of Formation: A Critique of Philosophy for Children 28

Part II Philosophy in Children: Affirmative Practices

5 Philosophy at Public Schools of Brasilia, DF 44

6 (Some) Reasons for Doing Philosophy with Children 61

7 *Philosophizing with Children* at a Philosophy Camp 75

8 Does Philosophy Fit in Caxias? A Latin
   American Project   87
9 Philosophy as Spiritual and Political Exercise in an
   Adult Literacy Course   97

Appendices   115
Bibliography   121
Index   126

Foreword

Walter Kohan's new book is addressed to students, teachers and anyone interested in the relationships among childhood, philosophy and education—all of whom will no doubt be challenged and inspired by what they find in these pages. Kohan's journey in the space where those three terms intersect is at once highly personal—even idiosyncratic—and of almost universal interest, animated as it is by the profound and perennial questions: What is Philosophy? What is Education? and What is Childhood? Kohan's work reveals that none of these questions can be engaged to any great extent without engaging the others at least to some extent. His fundamental thesis is that children's philosophical practice—with each other and with adults—has the potential to disrupt what we thought we knew about all three, and to enable children and adults together to reconstruct their meaning as well as the customs and institutions we mutually inhabit.

Kohan is an exemplar and champion of what Keats referred to as "negative capability"—the disposition not only to sustain ambiguity, uncertainty and wonder but also to resist solutions or answers that might close them off. For Kohan, the question that resists answering is not only a methodological commitment but also a normative principle for what it means to practice philosophy, childhood and education: "All attempts to complete philosophy fail: there is no way to foreclose the enigma of thinking, the mystery of what we are and what we could be. In doing philosophy we accompany that enigma, maintain it, feed it, but we cannot mitigate it."

As monotheist theologians, Taoist sages and leftist political theorists have demonstrated, the *via negativa* is fraught with paradox in theory and in action. One of the most important aspects of this book is the vital, creative tension it displays—on almost every page—between Kohan's own indications of new directions for the work of philosophy for children and his active mistrust of authoritative prescriptions for that work. On the one hand, for instance, he is intentionally vague about the purposes of this play/work: "We do not know what kinds of world will emerge from the encounter between philosophy, education and childhood—nor do we want to." On the other, his critique of the theory, practice and curriculum of philosophy for children generated by founders Matthew Lipman and Ann Margaret Sharp is situated in a broader critique of Brazilian and global economics and politics and the educational practices that help to maintain them—a critique that derives from specific ethical and political commitments.

Another location of this tension is the practice of philosophy and education we see Kohan inventing, which is coherent enough to be intentional but not so formal as to preclude un-thought-of possibilities. At the same time that he asserts that philosophy "escapes from any method," he allows that the efficacy of transformative philosophical practice depends on its instantiating principles including critical questioning, participative inquiry, democracy, solidarity and resistance to imposition. While he insists that philosophy in schools resists transmitting values, his work with students presupposes and enacts specific values that are, if not foundational then at least "not unfounded." In one sense Kohan's philosophical engagement with children and adults is anti-methodological; in another it is the object of methodical interrogation and reconstruction.

More broadly, Kohan invites us to "stop thinking of education as a training device to promote certain forms of subjectivity...and begin to think of it as a practice of opening spaces [where] teacher and students can take part in new forms, new becomings." He envisions educational spaces in which "children can think as openly, strongly, and freely as possible about what kind of world they want to live in," and in which adults have the opportunity to become uncultured and unlearned in the presence of that thinking—which is where philosophy begins. One tension here is that philosophical education that honors childhood as a source of radical trans-formation depends on a number of relatively stable forms, including a shared language, a shared commitment to openness and non-coercion, an agreement to mutual critique, and certain conditions of time, space, nutrition and so on. All of these forms enable as well as constrict, and to unlearn or become de-formed from them would disable as much as liberate.

The paradox of negative capability is most pressing when it comes to the fundamental philosophical question of how to live. Kohan reminds us that what makes a question philosophical is our capacity and willingness to let ourselves be questioned by it and to be transformed by our engagement with it: "Philosophical thinking is thinking that problematizes the given including, always, one's own life in relationship to the given." But he also stresses that the task of philosophy is to pose such problems, not to solve them; to inquire without seeking to know more but in fact "to know a little less." What, then, becomes of the person who unlearns how to live? What kind of insights might arise from such *aporia*? And how can new forms be worked out or played with in ways that leave them capable of being undone?

The creative vitality of all of these tensions is lost if we read them as simple distinctions—between freedom and discipline, purpose and neutrality, inquiry and mystery, indication and prescription, tradition and novelty—easily reconciled by giving each its due or by finding some middle path. The force of Kohan's thought and the great promise of his example comes from the fact that he has taken neither option. Rather, he has found new meanings in the opposition created by these distinctions. In this book he invites us to resist the temptation to resolve them and instead to inhabit them and reconsider our relationships to philosophy, childhood and education from their vantage.

Maughn Gregory
April 2014

Preface and Acknowledgments

This is a philosophical book on the education of childhood, or a childlike book on the education of philosophy. I am playing with words in that precise sense in which some children, sometimes, play so seriously: I am entirely in those words and I truly mean them. I genuinely mean that this is an educational book and that what is at sake is the relationship between childhood and philosophy through education. This is the way I inhabit the world of *philosophy for children* (p4c). My basic premise is that the encounter of childhood and philosophy calls for a rebirth of each, and of their relationship to the other.

This is the main idea I will try to unfold in this book. "Idea" does not mean here an abstract concept but a very concrete way of thinking that inhabits a way of living. This is why this book contains two parts: the first, "Philosophy for Children: Critical Perspectives," describes my own critical relationship to *philosophy for children*, to which I was introduced by Matthew Lipman and Ann Margaret Sharp. The chapters in this part aim to think through the educational possibilities of bringing philosophy, as collective inquiry, to children. The second part, "Philosophizing in Childhood: Affirmative Practices," describes alternative exercises of thinking and practicing this relationship I have undertaken over the past twenty years. In other words, the book travels from a program to a movement inaugurated by that program. In this sense, this book replicates my own path in the movement of philosophical experiences in childhood in the past twenty years.

Let me briefly describe this path. The first chapter of Part I, "Some Biographical Remarks and Philosophical Questions within Philosophy for Children," offers a philosophical questioning of the way p4c has traditionally conceptualized philosophy and the educational relationship that it presumes to cultivate between philosophy and children. The main issue discussed in this chapter is the way p4c answers the question: "What is philosophy?"—in particular, the role of questioning in philosophical inquiry and the political senses attributed to philosophy in p4c. The second chapter, "Celebrating Thirty Years of Philosophy for Children," concentrates on the way p4c answers the question "What is childhood?" The analysis of Greek notions of time (*chronos*, *kairos*, *aion*) here helps us reconsider the sovereignty of the chronological understanding of childhood that is so prevalent in educational discourse, including p4c. Chapter 3, "Good-Bye to Matthew Lipman (and Ann Margaret Sharp)," examines the values of the creators of p4c and of some of the biographical events that help us to understand their lives devoted to p4c. Chapter 4, "The Politics of Formation: A Critique of Philosophy for Children," offers a more educational and political critique of p4c, centered in a critique of the idea of formation. Starting from Plato's idea of the relationships among childhood, education and politics, it shows the birth of a continuous line of thought and practice, in which p4c surprisingly establishes itself.

The book's second part begins with Chapter 5, "Philosophy at Public Schools of Brasilia, DF," which describes a project of practicing philosophy with children in public schools of the Federal District of Brazil. It covers the theoretical, methodological and practical dimensions of this project and evaluates it as a teacher education proposal. Some parts of this chapter were co-authored with Rosana Fernandes. Chapter 6, "[Some] Reasons for Doing Philosophy with Children," offers reasons for doing philosophy with children, derived mainly from the testimony of children practicing philosophy in the project described in the previous chapter. This chapter focuses on a reconstruction of the idea of childhood and its educational condition, starting from the voices of children themselves. Chapter 7, "Philosophizing with Children at a Philosophy Camp," narrates an experience of educational philosophy the author undertook with Korean children at a philosophy camp in Seoul. After describing this experience, the chapter considers the meaning of doing philosophy with children everywhere, and questions some purposes commonly affirmed for this practice, in educational discourse: (a) education for citizenship; (b) forming people capable of an (intelligent) adaptation to the labor market; (c) something enjoyable in itself, which does not require other justification. Chapter 8, "Does Philosophy Fit in Caxias? A Latin American Project," describes a project of practicing philosophy with children in Duque de Caxias, Rio de Janeiro, Brazil, which is taking place at present (2014). These pages explore this project's creative and unique ways of educating children (and adults) through philosophical experiences of thinking. Finally, Chapter 9, "Philosophy as Spiritual and Political Exercise in an Adult Literacy Course," (co-authored with Jason Wozniak) explores the educational possibilities of an experience of philosophy with illiterate and marginalized students in a public school taking part in the same project described in the previous chapter. This chapter presents a practice of reconstruction of the childlike subject, who is not a chronological child but a chronological adult experiencing a childlike education through philosophy.

Throughout this book I am hoping to give some food for the thought of students, teachers and whoever is interested in the education of childhood through philosophy and, I reiterate, the education of philosophy through childhood. The chapters in this book have been written along a period of almost fifteen years. Most of them were not published in English as presented here. A previous and different version of Chapter 4 was published as "Education, Philosophy and Childhood" in *Thinking: The Journal of Philosophy for Children*, vol. 16, pp. 4–11, 2002. Chapter 8, "Does Philosophy Fit in Caxias? A Latin American Project," was published as a chapter in *Philosophy in Schools*, Sara Goering, Nicholas J. Shudak and Thomas E. Wartenberg (eds.). New York: Routledge, 2013, pp. 86–96. And Chapter 9, "Philosophy as Spiritual and Political Exercise in an Adult Literacy Course," was published in *Thinking: The Journal of Philosophy for Children*, vol. 19, pp. 17–23, 2010.

This book is a result of a journey of more than twenty years, since I got in touch with *philosophy for children* at the end of 1992, through the work of Gloria Arbones in Buenos Aires. I thank Matthew Lipman and Ann Margaret Sharp for their extraordinary generosity in opening the world of philosophical practices with children to me. Thanks to them, a new world of people and ideas has inspired my work and life ever since. The Brazilian Public Education System has given support to my research through my position as Full Professor at the State University of Rio de Janeiro and as Researcher of Foundations including FAPERJ (Fundação de Amparo à Pesquisa do Estado do Rio de Janeiro [Support for Research of the State of Rio de Janeiro]) and CNPq (Conselho Nacional de Desenvolvimento Científico e Tecnológico [the National Council of Scientific and Technological Research]). My colleagues and students at the Center of Philosophical Studies on Childhood (NEFI) at the State University of Rio de Janeiro have been challenging and inspiring interlocutors of my ideas for the past twelve years. David Kennedy has always been a dear friend, philosophical companion and someone who has helped with my English. Palgrave Macmillan's series editor Gert Biesta has been very supportive of this project. Maughn Gregory has honored me with his Foreword. Less evidently but no less importantly, conversations with a number of friends in different countries have given inspiration and form to these pages throughout the past twenty years. I dedicate this book to the students and teachers of the schools of Duque de Caxias, Rio de Janeiro, Brasil.

Walter Omar Kohan
Rio de Janeiro, March, 2014

Part I
Philosophy for Children:
Critical Perspectives

1
Some Biographical Remarks and Philosophical Questions within Philosophy for Children

Abstract: *This chapter offers a philosophical questioning of the way p4c has traditionally conceptualized philosophy and the educational relationship that it presumes to cultivate between philosophy and children. The main issue discussed in this chapter is the way p4c answers the question: "what is philosophy?"—in particular, the role of questioning in philosophical inquiry and the political senses attributed to philosophy in p4c.*

Keywords: education as formation; Matthew Lipman; Philosophy for Children; Plato; thinking; what is philosophy?

Kohan, Walter Omar. *Philosophy and Childhood: Critical Perspectives and Affirmative Practices.* New York: Palgrave Macmillan, 2014. DOI: 10.1057/9781137469175.0005.

I was already in love with philosophy when I fell in love with Philosophy for Children (p4c) in the early 1990s—perhaps similar to Matthew Lipman, the creator of p4c, who fell in love with philosophy in the 1950s and with education in the 1960s. My first wonder then turned into admiration for what seemed to be a radically different conception both of philosophy and of education.

Those initial feelings were deepened as I made personal contact with Matthew Lipman, Ann Sharp and other colleagues in different parts of the world. Entering the world of p4c meant living in a space consecrated to serious educational and philosophical change. They were years of deep dedication, study and practice with Lipman's paradigm. I worked with children and adults especially from diverse countries in Latin America—mainly in Argentina, Brazil, Chile, Mexico and Uruguay. In 1996 I completed my Ph.D. in p4c at Iberoamericana University in Mexico City, with a thesis mentored by Lipman and Ronald Reed—that warm friend, died a couple of years later. From 1997 to 2002 I have taught in the Faculty of Education of the University of Brasilia, where I coordinated the project "Filosofia na Escola," to bring the practice of philosophy to public school children and teachers in the Federal District of Brazil. Since 2002 I do a similar work in the State University of Rio de Janeiro, where we develop an analogous project in the city of Duque de Caxias, a suburb of Rio.

Much time, experiences and practices have passed and while still in love with Lipman's project, I have increasingly felt the need to re-create its themes from other bases. My own practice with children and educators, as well as being in touch with diverse institutions created all around the world to "disseminate" the program, have consolidated in me strong beliefs about the educational possibilities of the practice of philosophy with children and teachers and, at the same time, serious doubts (philosophical, educational, political) regarding the benefits of the application of the Institute for the Advancement of Philosophy for Children (IAPC) model and, most generally, p4c methodology and theoretical principles—at least in Latin American countries, where I have worked most. As in all forms of philosophical love, the questions, the critique, the differences, cannot be absent, and, in my case, quite the contrary, they have deepened over the years. In this brief introductory chapter, I will try to expose some of those doubts and present my basis for them as well.

1.1 Philosophical questions

I consider Lipman's project, p4c, to be potentially revolutionary—not only for philosophy and education, but for childhood as well—both theoretically and practically. Although different thinkers in different times have pointed out children's philosophical potential, no one before Lipman has attributed such a primary place for them in the world of philosophical ideas concerning education. Characteristic of someone deeply shaped by the pragmatist philosophical and educational tradition, Lipman not only speculated about these ideas, but also created a methodology that turned them into a reality. The expansion of his program into so many countries today is a sign of the strength of his ideas and his practices.

As pretended by Lipman, I consider p4c a philosophical adventure and as such I offer to it the highest honor a philosopher can receive, which is to debate the assumptions and implications of his thought and practice. Unfortunately p4c has provoked more apologies and attacks than critical attention. Paradoxically, both who defend and attack it, either by considering p4c a salvation for education or a non-philosophical pedagogy, with that gesture group themselves outside philosophy. Far from these two positions, I will outline some of my queries. Because of the deepness of the issues involved, I will just present them acknowledging that they call for greater development elsewhere.

1.2 Can philosophy be taught? If so, how should it be taught?

This first question might recall Kant's classic dichotomy concerning the impossibility of learning philosophy. Let's remember it: it is impossible to learn philosophy as an accomplished discipline, only to *philosophize* can be learned (*Critique of Pure Reason*, B 865–9). Even though the dichotomy can be overcome considering that practice always calls for theory and that it is not possible to exercise philosophical thinking without philosophy as theory taking place in some way, it would still be important to question whether the *learning* of philosophy—the experience of philosophizing—can actually be taught in institutions such as schools.

Lipman just presupposes an affirmative answer to this question, without even considering it. Let us accept, for the moment, this position: let's consider *as if* philosophy—the experience of it—could be taught in

Lipman's terms: to teach philosophy to children is to reconstruct the history of philosophy in such a why as to provoke children's philosophizing through it. New questions emerge: How should we teach philosophy to provoke children's philosophizing? Is there a best—more useful, true, effective—form of doing so? Can this question be solved through pedagogical, technical or scientific means? Lipman seems to respond to all of these questions affirmatively. His answer is obvious: his program, p4c, is that best form. Moreover, it is the only attempt that has reconstructed philosophy in its integrity and complexity so that children could really experience it in communities of philosophical inquiry. By doing this, he considers that the community of philosophical inquiry contributes and approximates the conditions of "an ideal speech situation," where "formal properties of discourse" would give the key elements to decide on the excellence in argumentation (Lipman, 2001: 414). Under this form, a kind of Hegelianism (through Dewey's influence) appears in this reconstruction of the history of philosophy: philosophy seems to have reached its realized form as a teachable discipline in p4c. In other words, p4c represents a culminating didactic resource, overcoming all previous ones to bring Philosophy for Children.

Let's examine this pretension. What sort of philosophy does p4c introduce to the young? How does Lipman respond to the question "What is philosophy?" Lipman considers philosophy as a form of thinking. In his first writings, such as *Philosophy in the Classroom* (1980), *Philosophy Goes to School* (1988) and the first edition of *Thinking of Education* (1991) only two forms of thinking are considered: critical and creative. Progressively, he acknowledges a third dimension, caring, thoroughly explored in the second edition of *Thinking in Education* (Lipman, 2003). Lipman also considers philosophy as distributed thinking and, no less important, as a form of self-corrective questioning, logical and dialogical inquiry (ibid.: 408–9). All these formulations have extraordinary dimensions. Just as an example of a more thorough task, here I am only going to problematize the role assigned by Lipman to questioning.

I could not agree more with Lipman about the importance of questioning as the "leading edge of [philosophical] inquiry" (ibid.: 410–1). Philosophy arises from a question, and lives in the questions that develop from, modify and renovate that initial question. Just as philosophy would be little without its questions, a philosophical experience that didn't exercise them would be an impoverished one. Nevertheless, we find that Lipman's emphasis on questioning appears to be reduced in its possibilities in at least three senses: in its scope, in its conception and in the form in which it is exercised. Let me try to present why.

Again, what is the meaning of questioning in philosophy? It is through questions that philosophical inquiry moves to expand the problematic dimension of our being in the world. In philosophy alone, of all the disciplines, do our questions turn into self-questioning, into placing ourselves—our own subjectivity, both individual and social—into question. We don't ask philosophical questions to seek information, even knowledge or anything external to us, even though we can gain any of these; rather, we are committed in the question within the question. We wonder. We put ourselves into questions. We let questions go through our thinking and life. It is for this reason that in philosophy it is impossible to ask for another—to ask someone else's question, to just repeat anyone else's question. The one who repeats the question of another one is not questioning anything, strictly speaking, much less is he or she self-questioning; he or she is merely reproducing someone else's inquietude. Therefore it is important that children and teachers question and self-question, so that they can find the extraordinary in the ordinary, the arbitrary in the natural, the complex in the simple, the contingent in the obvious. Collective philosophical inquiry always expands the field of the problematic in us, to us, within us. If, as Lipman says, the inquiry "seeks to render a problematic situation no longer problematic" (ibid.: 412), then it stops being philosophical. The major characteristic of living a philosophical life is its capacity to put itself into question, in posing problems to its life, not in solving its problems. In philosophy we do not really question to know more about whatever but, mainly, to stop knowing—to know a little less, to just know we do not know, to put it in Socratic terms. I do not mean that in philosophy we ask just for the sake of asking, nor that no questions could be answered or no answers could be affirmed. Much less, that answers do not count at all. Of course they do and through philosophical inquiry much attention is given to examine alternative answers to a problem. But philosophical thinking means primarily thinking through questions that are posed directly to our own life or thinking, or to different values, concepts and knowledge affirmed in other fields—such as politics, art, religion, science—that inform our own life and thinking. It questions the unquestioned assumptions, thus revises its conditions and opens them to alternative possibilities.

Traditionally philosophy has been rooted in wonder or, as Jaspers (1959) put it, in three feelings: wonder, doubt and commotion, and the consciousness of being lost by human beings. Even though I acknowledge these possibilities I prefer to add a fourth one: dissatisfaction, which I think is specifically significant in an economic, social and political environment such as Latin America. In this sense, dissatisfaction that provokes philosophical questioning in this context has two main characteristics: first, it springs from a state of things that urges and calls for problematization, and second, it never conforms. Philosophical questions can be answered in many different ways, but no answer can mitigate the intensity of the dissatisfaction that sustains them. It is in this intensity that the problems and concepts of philosophy emerge. I don't believe that philosophy can be found, as Lipman (2001: 406) has suggested in a body of abstract, complex, general and ill-defined ideas. Questions lead to problems. Not every question contains a problem but a philosophical problem emerges and is expressed in the form of a question. Problems and concepts in philosophy are as historical as the people who produce them. Although we have many words in common with the Greeks, the medieval and other philosophical traditions, and even though we can be sharing the form of some questions, the meanings of those words and questions that arise of them change substantially over time, so that different situated philosophical problems emerge.

Let's take an example. Although we still consider truth as a philosophical problem, the Greek philosophers asked what truth is in an absolute way, tying to find out something like its essence, nature or character. Today we are not as interested in what truth is as in how it works, how it is produced, legitimated and transmitted through diverse contemporary social devices (as diverse of those of the classic Greeks) assuming its not absolute character. Greek philosophers gave different answers to what truth is while now we seem to be more interested in problematizing the effect of any social dispositive to produce truth. For the Greeks the nature of truth was a question in itself. For the Greeks truth was discovered while for us it is produced, invented, something that would appear, at the very least, banal or danger to Plato or Aristotle or even relativists such as Protagoras. Thus the problems of philosophy can be neither universalized nor anticipated, much less foreseen.

From this example, we can question to what extent a history of philosophy (a history of *the* questions, concepts and problems of philosophy) reconstructed *à la Lipman*—which, by the way, doesn't cover developments over the past thirty years, much less significant previous ones—is such an interesting way to encourage children's philosophical questions.

DOI: 10.1057/9781137469175.0005

In other words, what sorts of questions, and what further development of those questions, would such a reconstruction favor if not *the* abstract, general and fundamental questions, *the* common, central and controversial questions that p4c considers the questions of all time philosophy? Is this the most interesting way to help children to find their questions and problems and put their own thinking and life into question?

Furthermore, we can question Lipman's (2001: 410) novels and manuals as they are proposed to be models of philosophical inquiry. In fact nothing seems less philosophical than the so-called philosophical manual—no matter how many questions and how few answers it contains—because a manual by definition constitutes a kind of answer to how philosophy ought to be taught, and how questions should be asked. The idea of a manual presupposes that at least in some sense philosophy can be transmitted, taught didactically. In this way, it injures the very dimension of philosophical experience (open, problematic, non-transferable) that it instructs us in. In its presentation through manuals, philosophical questioning appears as being external to its practitioners. I wonder whether the manuals don't create an external relationship, not only to the practicing philosophical subjects it addresses (children and educators), but to their own questions as well.

1.3 Why teach philosophy? What are the relationships among philosophy, education and politics?

At least, since Plato's *The Republic*, the aim of education is to make of what it is to what it ought to be. Education is thus placed as the way to turn an unfair *pólis* into a fair one. Since then, the education of children has been a privileged tool in the political utopias of our historical past. We do this with the best of intentions, of course. As Lipman says, "these are our children and we want only good things to happen to them" (2001: 411).

With all his anti-Platonism inherited from John Dewey, Lipman seems to accept this scheme without question. He wants education to insure that children will be "good people" (ibid.). It is for this reason that he introduces philosophy into their education—as a tool used to promote the formation of more critical, reasonable, democratic, tolerant, judicious people (Lipman, 2001). He considers the teaching of philosophy to be a key to education for democracy. He would probably accept that there would be no need to teach philosophy if it didn't lead us there or if we were already at such a place. The teaching of philosophy is grounded and given meaning, for Lipman, in a socio-political logic—not a philosophical one. He intends to educate children in philosophy in order to consolidate the democratic utopian dream.

It is amazing how the way of linking the relationship between philosophy, education and politics is so close to a traditional form in a program, such as Philosophy for Children, that presents itself as so different from "traditional philosophy." Although it changes the final political aim of education to that of deliberative democracy, the pillars of traditional education remain: the goals of the enterprise are defined by an architecture external to philosophy itself, a logic previous and external to those involved in the educational process itself—children and teachers. It still considers education as what might bring as from what it is to what ought to be. Sure, it ruminates philosophy in a very different way, from knowledge to communal inquiry, and it changes the political goal of education from the aristocratic polis to the deliberative democracy, but the logic of the relationship between philosophy, education and politics does not change so much: an educational philosophy will enable to achieve the deserved political order.

In this sense p4c would not appear to offer much of a revolutionary philosophical and educational alternative to current institutions and structures if inspired by the Platonic Model. If we consider philosophy as a form of really transformative thinking it should not have any fixed arriving points: democracy, tolerance, critique and philosophy itself are problems—questions to be thought. This doesn't mean that philosophy and education don't assume any political commitment, or that they are apolitical. Rather, it assumes a commitment to rethink their political dimension, to locate the relationships between philosophy and politics in a philosophical, not political, space.

Philosophy's political potential resides within philosophy itself—in the power of a form of questioning which is transformative. Philosophy affirms a transformative *means*: unrestricted questioning. All it promises is the opportunity to wonder—to question the ideas, knowledge and values affirmed in the state of things, and our relationship to those affirmations. It opens the spaces of education so that its subjects can ask and wonder about the world they inhabit in such a way that, through the experience of philosophy, these subjects can no longer think in the same way before philosophizing. The outcomes of those transformations do not need to be decided in advance. A transformative education might have some commitments in terms of the forms of practice affirmed, but no pre-decided point of arrival.

If the desacralizing power of philosophy has always been important—as shown by philosophers as various as Socrates, Nietzsche and Foucault—it seems even more important in the present context, in which a sacralized and unquestioned ideology of representative democracy, "free" market and legalized human rights is imposed everywhere in a manner insensitive to cultural differences, thus reinforcing social exclusion and inequality.

1.4 Final remarks

These are just a few of the issues that Lipman's formidable proposal invites and foster us to think. Others could also be brought into question. Among them are the relationship between logic and philosophy (and between logic and ethics in particular); the conception of logic affirmed in the program; the understanding of the institution of the school that the program presupposes; the personal ideals affirmed in the characters of the novels; the assumption that community of inquiry is an ideal model for education; the idea of philosophical modeling that the program puts forth; the claims made about the relationship between philosophy and other disciplines, especially literature; Lipman's "child," or the way of conceiving the child and what is expected of him or her; the role assigned to the teacher in the philosophical discussion; the institutional form that has assumed the diffusion of the program throughout the world; the role that the program plays in the current educational reforms in Latin America and other regions of the world.

In this chapter I have for the most part affirmed my relationship with Lipman's program, while trying to point out that if is to be a truly philosophical venture into education, it demands a truly philosophical posture. It demands the prevalence of the question. As long as p4c's answers hide its questions, the movement might be able to impact educational systems, but the philosophical, educational and political force of that impact will be seriously affected.

2
Celebrating Thirty Years of Philosophy for Children

Abstract: *This chapter concentrates on the way p4c answers the question "What is childhood?" The analysis of Greek notions of time (chronos, kairos, aion) helps us reconsider the sovereignty of the chronological understanding of childhood that is so prevalent in educational discourse, including p4c.*

Keywords: childhood; experience; Manoel de Barros; Philosophy for Children; teacher education; time

Kohan, Walter Omar. *Philosophy and Childhood: Critical Perspectives and Affirmative Practices.* New York: Palgrave Macmillan, 2014. DOI: 10.1057/9781137469175.0006.

There are so many things to celebrate about Philosophy for Children! Where to focus? Where to begin? How to choose the most appropriate words, images, and style? Let's bet on philosophy: yes, I'll do my best to write a philosophical celebration of the thirty years of the IAPC. I'll concentrate on the concept of childhood.

My starting point is a series of memories. I've spent extended time at the IAPC on at least four occasions. I am saying "at least" in order to give opportunity to other forms of experience that my conscious memory does not allow me at this moment. The first two were directly related to my participation in two introductory workshops at Mendham in May and August, 1993. I also shared another Mendham, this time as a "coach," during my third stay at the IAPC, the most memorable one, when I had the honor and happiness to be close to Matthew Lipman while writing the final version of my PhD dissertation. My fourth and final visit to the IAPC was in June 2002, when I took part in a North American Association for the Community of Inquiry (NAACI) conference.

It's interesting to note how the *momentum*, individual and social, we are living in a given time and space mediates the relationship we establish with the places through which we pass. The "same" context might be experienced in very different ways, partly because a place is never the same, and partly because we human beings are always in movement. These remarks sound particularly meaningful for a traveler. To travel means to move in space and time, and to experience difference—at least for those, like me, for whom transformation is a meaningful idea—and this might (or might not) turn into a transformative experience. I am aware that in many cases this transformation does not happen, particularly in societies such as ours, which seem to be especially efficient in impoverishing experience. I am referring particularly to the impoverishment of the experience of travel—for example, those professional lecturers who travel just to repeat the same thing to different audiences, and return to their place being nearly the same as they were when they began the trip. In a number of ways they could be said to stay in the same "place" (of beliefs, ideas, or convictions) and are not very ready to challenge their convictions, even though they might physically be dislocating themselves by dozens or thousands of miles. But there are also those travelers who start on a trip as someone who is entering an opportunity to transform his or her own subjectivity, through opening himself or herself to difference. These are the kinds of voyages where the traveler does not know at the start or even in the middle of the journey at which destiny he or she will arrive.

For me, to travel has always been this kind of opportunity. My dislocations to the IAPC in particular have meant an extraordinary opportunity to transform what I thought, the values I appreciated and, most important, who I was. I have seen the IAPC very differently in my different visits, partly because of its own changes and movements, and partly because of mine. I felt very different on all these occasions, as I am probably feeling differently now, from other previous occasions.

My first two experiences in Mendham were really impressive. Mendham is probably one of IAPC's most distinctive contributions to the world of education and philosophy. It is difficult to find another place where the experience of philosophy is so intensive and so coherently taken with the theoretical and methodological assumptions of the enterprise. It is difficult to find another place where philosophy is a means to really transform what we think and the way we live.

Mendham is a symbol of the fully lived experience of philosophy, and we probably haven't yet been able to perceive how important Mendham could be for the philosophical world of our time—as a full experience of philosophy, with all its complexities. What is it that really happens in Mendham? How might we name it? I am not so sure. I would prefer not to call it dialogue, given that I am not so sure about the kind of interchange that really takes place between these people from very different histories, cultures, formation, aspirations, and languages that during two weeks concentrate themselves on thinking philosophy, childhood, and education. But one point rests strongly enough: anyone who passes through Mendham has a great opportunity never to think or be the same after it. Mendham is a place of transformative experience. This is precisely one of the characteristics of philosophical thinking: it never leaves things as they were before.

Mendham's quasi-isolation from the outside world and the way every concrete, material need is facilitated helps every participant to concentrate just on philosophy and education. All these conditions really make the place very seductive and stimulating for philosophical thinking.

Nevertheless, it's not all flowers at Mendham. The "Mecca" of p4c is a very complex place. On the one hand, Mendham is a place of transformation through theory and practice. At Mendham, philosophy is done and experienced in a very deep and powerful form. People are not here just to "say" what they think, in other words, to speculate about "philosophical dialogue" or inquiry, but to undertake dialogue and inquiry themselves! The difference is not minor.

At the same time, this brightness also leaves some shadows. Mendham is so separated and isolated from the "real" world; it provides such an ideal environment, that it is not so easy to see how it will ever be possible to approximate—even a little—both worlds. This sort of dualism which Mendham echoes seems to me to be part of a deeper one that goes through all of p4c—its methodology, its curriculum of novels and manuals, its aims, its understanding of what school is, of what a child is, of what philosophy is: a kind of visceral and dramatic dualism between what it is and what it ought to be. It is true that this dualism is, in a sense, inherent to a whole philosophical tradition, at least from Plato to modern times. But this fact does not reduce its impact. Anyhow, I've promised to write a celebratory paper focusing on the concept of childhood, and that's what I am going to do.

I cannot describe with words the generosity with which Matthew Lipman and Ann Margaret Sharp have always received me at the IAPC. This generosity was particularly remarkable in 1995, when I came to write my dissertation. Mentored by Lipman, I had the privilege to visit him as many times as I needed, "most preferably during the morning, given that my eyes are getting tired" as Mat suggested. In Lipman I have always found a person ready to help me—reading my drafts nearly instantly and giving me, in few words, the kind of philosophical and human support that is so rare to find in the academy. I could not be luckier. It was a real privilege.

Let's go now to childhood. There are so many concepts of childhood surrounding the history of philosophy and education. The most dominant view has some clear markers: a non-reversible, sequential. and consecutive concept of chronology, a continuous and progressive notion of development, and a dichotomist meaning of potentiality. In effect, in this paradigm, human life is understood as a unity divided into periods or stages, each of which has some specific features. A human being is first a fetus, then a baby, child, adolescent, teen-ager, and so on. The movement ascends in various dimensions: epistemological, ethical, political. Children are potential adults and adults have been once children. There is no way to be an adult without being first a child; there is no way to be a child once you turn into an adult. I beg the reader's pardon for such simplistic and obvious scheme—this is not the place to analyze it in all its complexities—but this simple description will take me directly to the point I want to discuss. More interestingly, it's being so obvious and natural is precisely a significant part of the problem.

Usually this line is seen as progressive, and childhood is considered negative in relation to adulthood. But it could also be the other way around, as in Romanticism. Contemporary Brazilian poet, Manoel de Barros, published a very nice book of narratives on childhood entitled *Invented Memories: Childhood* (Barros, 2010). The title might sound a little strange: memory is typically understood as a capacity to remember the past, usually associated with discovery and recognition, but not with invention; and invention is usually connected with the future, to the opening of a new beginning, a new point of departure. "Invented memories" is something the grammarians call an oxymoron—two terms in contradiction. If something is invented, then it could not be a memory; if something is a memory then it could not be an invention, at least according to the usual meanings of these words. Other examples of oxymoron might be "hot ice-cream," "small ocean," or "experienced child." In each case the meaning of one term seems to be in contradiction to the other.

The place of contradictions in thinking is not so simple. On the one hand, they render us unable to think, and that's why Aristotle has given us a logical principle of non-contradiction. In a sense, they are unthinkable, such as black holes for thinking. At the same time they are a stimulus or even a condition for thinking. There would be very little to think in a non-contradictory world.

Invented Memories has a nice epigraph that helps us to think in terms of the contradiction posed by the title of the book: "All that I do not invent is false." Let's pay this phrase some closer attention (with compliments to Harry Stottlemeier): it is not that every invention is true, but that, to be true, something needs to be invented. Now the title takes on a new meaning: if anything true needs to be invented, then there is no chance that memories could not be invented if we want them to be true and not false. So the contradiction helps us to think: memory might be seen not only as a faculty which allows us to bring the past to the present, but also as a capacity to invent a new present, at any time. *Invented Memories* invents a new concept of memory in its very title.

The book has sixteen short memories. I'll dwell a bit on memory fourteen, entitled "Achadouros." This is a very difficult word to translate. It was invented by the poet and comprises two Portuguese words—"achado" which comes from the verb "'achar," meaning "to find," and "ouro" which means "gold." "Achadouros" would be something like "places where gold could be found." The memory speaks of those Dutch who came to Brazil in search of gold and occasionally left in a hurry, leaving behind them some sort of trunks full of gold. The poet says he is a hunter for childhood, and he looks for places which are full of childhood as trunks are full of gold. Through this example he tells us what he is trying to find in childhood. When we are children, he says, everything looks bigger than when we are adults. Consider, for example, the yard behind our house. In our childhood it looks like the biggest yard in the world, and the more we "grow up" the smaller it looks. Some people might say that this is very simple to explain, that it is a matter of perspective; but the poet offers a different explanation: "it's a matter if intimacy," he says. The more intimate we are with something, the bigger it will look: "the size of a thing depends on the intimacy we have with it" (Barros, 2010: 14). Like love, like thinking, like philosophy, it is—before anything else—a matter of intimacy. Childhood, chronological childhood, is time (*chronos*) of intimate relationships with the world. Entering into adulthood means impoverishing this kind of intimacy.

There are a number of philosophical assumptions underlying this anthropology. There are many underlying answers to philosophical questions and concepts such as time, life, space, and so on. Let's consider one of these, the concept of time.

The Ancient Greeks had many words to refer to time. One of those is *chronos*, which mentors the continuity of successive time. Plato defines *chronos* as "the moving image of eternity (*aion*) that moves according to number" (*Timeus*, 37d). For the Athenian, who was so attracted by dualities, there are two kinds of worlds: one is the world of immutability, eternity, perfection; there is also a moving world, subject to generation and corruption, imperfect, the world we live in; we numerate the natural movement in this world and we call it *chronos*. So for the Athenian, time, as *chronos*, is only possible in this imperfect world due to one of its most imperfect marks: movement. The perfect world of ideas is ana-chronic, has no chronic time. Some decades later, Aristotle, who did not seem to accept Plato's split into two worlds, defined *chronos*, without a model, as "the number of movement according to the 'before and after'" *Physics* (IV, 220a). *Chronos*-time is then the sum of past, present, and future, and the present is a limit between time that has already been but that is not any more (past) and time that has not yet come into being, even though it will (future). In this concept, the being of time is a limit between what is not anymore and what is not yet.

Even though *chronos* was the most successful and dominant word for time in the so called Western tradition, it is not the only one to speak about time among the Greeks. Another is *kairos*, which means "measure," "proportion" and, in relation to time, "critical time," "season," "opportunity" (Liddell & Scott, 1966: 859). A third word is *aion*, the same that Plato uses to refer himself to eternity in the quoted passage of *Timeus*; in its most ancient occurrences, *aion* designates the intensity of time in human life, a destiny, a duration, a un-numbered movement, not successive, but intense (ibid.: 45). If *chronos* is limit, *aion* is duration.

It might be interesting to go back to the childhood of this notion of time, especially to a time where philosophy was still not marked by the kind of divisions between its different realms which Aristotle inaugurated (i.e., epistemology, ethics, politics). Let's go then to the chronological childhood of philosophy. Before Plato, we find an instigating and powerful fragment from Heraclitus (DK 22 B 52) in which he connects this time-word with power and childhood. The fragment literally says, "*aion* is a child playing [literally, 'childing'], its realm is one of a child, childish." There is a double relationship affirmed in this fragment: time-childhood (*aion-pais*) and power-childhood (*basileíe-pais*). This difficult text seems to mean, among other things, that time—life-time—is not only a question of numbered movement, and that there is another way of living time that could be seen as a childlike way of being, one that belongs to a child. If one logic of time—the logic of *chronos*—moves according to numbers, another—that of *aion*—plays with movement.

Heraclitus' fragment also suggests that childhood is not just a period, a numbered or quantifiable phase of human life, but a realm that has intensity as one of its most remarkable marks. In this childlike realm that is time, there is no succession or consecutiveness, but just the intensity of duration (*aion*). A childlike force, a childlike power, Heraclitus suggests, is the realm of *aionic* time. It also allows us to think that childhood, much more than a stage of life, is a possibility of human experience, a potency, and a vital force.

Rebellion against chronological time and the notion of history it supports has been constant, mainly in philosophy and literature. Argentinean poet Jorge Luis Borges, like many others, condemned the modern slavery to history, which he called "one of the deepest sins of our epoch." He created a journal called *Destiempo* ("Un-time"). He dreamed, like Plato, of a time outside time, a non-commensurable instant where past, present, and future join (Borges, 1974: 706–9).

Gilles Deleuze, a contemporary French philosopher, distinguishes between two dimensions of time: history and *devenir* (becoming; Deleuze, 1990: 267). He describes them as two lines meeting in a single plane, or world. One is the consecutive and successive line of history that makes possible or follows experience. History is the conditions and the effects of experience. But experience is not explained or determined by history. History is the realm of causes and effects, and thus we can never predict or anticipate experience which is, in itself, unpredictable. Any explanation of real experience according to its historical causes is at the very least partial. History is continuous; experience is discontinuous, creative, and transformative. Experience interrupts history and introduces a new beginning to it: this is what he calls *devenir*.

Even though this analysis might look dualistic, Deleuze in fact combats the kind of dualism inaugurated by Plato. Both dimensions—history and experience—belong to the same and unique world; they are both immanent. The world is both history and experience; the lines cross each other on different planes constantly, in a complex movement. Going back to Heraclitus, we could say that history and experience denote two different dimensions of time, one chronological and the other *aionic*—numbered movement and un-numbered intensity. The same could be said of space. There is a measured space, one that numbers distance according to different scales: centimeters, meters, kilometers, and so on. This is *topos*, and there is also the intense space of *chora*: the intimate, not- measured space.

In this sense there are also at least two different childhoods. On the one side, we have the childhood of chronology and history; on the other, the childhood of *aion* and experience. Giorgio Agamben, a contemporary Italian philosopher, offers some powerful ideas in this respect, particularly in a book entitled *Childhood and History* (2000/1978). According to the etymology of the word "infant," childhood is basically an absence of speech. In effect, *in-fantia* references the lack of speech; the infant is the being incapable of speaking. On this purported absence many others have been based, and a whole negative anthropology of childhood has been founded.

However, Agamben points out that what is seen as a lack might also be seen as a capacity, condition, or affirmation (2000/1978: 17–82). In effect, if it is true that a child is born without that language characteristic of adults (and I do not want to get into another line of argumentation which might suggest that children have "other" languages), it is not less true that it is only when we are children that we can learn that language. In other words, childhood is needed in order to learn to speak and no adult can learn to speak if he or she had not done so in his or her childhood: there are only children—not adults—who learn to speak. And history and experience are much related to language: without childhood there would be no language, and without language there would be no history and no experience. Without childhood, humanity would be pure nature. Could you imagine a human being that would know how to speak when born, a kind of being with language inscribed in her genetic code? That would not be a human being.

So, childhood is a condition of possibility of adulthood, not only chronologically but also aionically. Childhood is a condition of possibility for humanity, for transformation, for the emergence of a difference in the world—for the new, whatever we might understand by that.

The two kinds of childhood have now more precise descriptors: chronology establishes the idea of history, development, and/or potentiality. This notion of childhood is based on a negative anthropology: children as lack. The other childhood (experience, transformation, and intensity) is based on an affirmative anthropology. I am not trying to condemn one and uphold the other. I am not judging, nor do I suggest we should replace one by the other or anything like that. Both are co-extensive, contemporaries, inter-actual.

What does all this have to do with p4c, with the IAPC, and with celebrating its 30th anniversary? Well, I hope some meaningful connections can be established. I'll only suggest a few. It seems quite clear that the most dominant concept of childhood underlying the enterprise of p4c is a chronological/developmental one. I do not want to question the importance of this concept, but I think there are some others that might enlarge and strengthen it and, together with it, would offer a new dimension to the whole enterprise of p4c. In a sense p4c is very traditional in its pedagogical aims: philosophy should go to schools to educate children, to turn them into democratic adults, responsible citizens.

All this might seem very important and meaningful from an adult perspective. No doubt it appears to be a noble task, especially in societies such as ours where there is no real democracy and no real citizenship. But on the other hand, we might wonder whether all these proposals for reform are not in fact functions of the very system they propose to reform; we might wonder whether all these well-intended aims are strong enough to establish at least some of the radical conditions our societies need in order to be transformed. Because it is not just a question of details or secondary characteristics of the system that need to be overcome. Our societies explode with injustice, inhumanity, lack of beauty. The kinds of transformations it needs are extremely radical. Nor am I thinking of any specific system that should or might replace the one we have. We need something deeper than a change of system—we need a change which leads us and allows us to recognize and honor all the different forms of life, individual and social. The problem is not only social fascism—the fascism of the dominant systems or of other systems. It is not only that what is socially called democratic is in fact fascist. It is more than that. As French thinker M. Foucault has pointed out, the problem is not exclusive or not mainly outside. It's inside (Foucault, 1977) We need to confront and seek to change *our* fascism, the fascism in our own thinking, the fascism that makes us think for the others, in the name of the others, against the others. If we think about it this way, we might wonder whether we ourselves are more fascistic than we would be ready to admit.

It seems to me that if we intend to think in a positive and at the same time non-fascist manner the concepts of thinking, philosophy, education, and childhood, then we need to recreate those concepts, and we would benefit by opening all of them to fully affirmative reconstruction. Accordingly, I have attempted here a short exercise with the concept of childhood. Nor have I chosen childhood accidentally. In a sense, we need to pursue, to hunt a new childhood, not a chronological one, so that philosophy and education could experience new beginnings. A new intensity, an intimacy with childhood can lead us to a new intensity in philosophy and education. In this sense, it is at least as important to bring children and childhood to philosophy as it is to bring philosophy to children and childhood. Of course, you might be thinking that it is not necessarily chronological children whom we need to bring to philosophy, but people who have decided to open themselves to a new kind of thinking, to thinking the new. If so, both enterprises could work together and bringing philosophy to children and childhood could be a nice way to bring children and childhood to philosophy.

These are my celebratory memories, memories that do not remember but invent. Intense memories. Memories of a child. Childish, childlike memories. Memories in childhood. Intimate, intense, memories. I hope that they can be meaningful to the reader and to his or her own way of thinking about p4c. I hope they might encounter the reader's childhood, wherever it is found. And I offer deep tribute to p4c, no matter how old it is, for it's aionic childhood.

3
Good-Bye to Matthew Lipman (and Ann Margaret Sharp)

Abstract: *This chapter examines the values of the creators of p4c and of some of the biographical events that help us to understand their lives devoted to p4c. It offers a reconstruction of Lipman's life from his own autobiography.*

Keywords: Ann Margaret Sharp; autobiography; homage; Matthew Lipman; Pablo Neruda; Philosophy for Children

Kohan, Walter Omar. *Philosophy and Childhood: Critical Perspectives and Affirmative Practices.* New York: Palgrave Macmillan, 2014. DOI: 10.1057/9781137469175.0007.

Toward the end of 2010, Matthew Lipman and Ann Margaret Sharp, creators of Philosophy for Children, passed away. Both were strong philosophers and educators committed to reforming educational institutions through the practice of philosophy. They came through a pragmatist tradition and their main contribution was the place they gave to philosophy in the education of childhood. It was not only a theoretical place, but one for which they deeply traveled the world and created a number of institutions in order to see it in practice.

At the time of his death Mat was living in an assisted living facility and dealing with deteriorating health mainly due to Parkinson's Disease. In his final years he could hardly work—much less than he desired, workaholic that he was—but he was still able to write his autobiography (2008) and give an interview to David Kennedy (2010) concerning Ann Sharp's passing.

Details of Lipman's life can be found in his autobiography, written just before Parkinson's Disease prevented him from writing at all. Son of immigrants from Eastern Europe, Matthew Lipman was born in Vineland, New Jersey. He spent his two first years in Philadelphia and then lived his childhood in Woodbirne, a small village of 2,000 inhabitants mainly comprising Russian immigrant farmers who came to the United States between the nineteenth and twentieth centuries. His paternal grandmother, Baba, took the family to the United States, after having lived in Germany and Siberia. Lipman's father, Wolf, was born in Germany. Wolf, different than the rest of his siblings who led agricultural lives, became a machinist, and was also an inventor who possessed a number of patents. In his frequent visits to his father's shop Lipman nurtured a propensity for practical things which, he affirms, he maintained for the rest of his life, professing a "prejudiced preference for practice over theory" (2008: 11). Lipman's mother, Sophie Kenin, of Jewish-Lithuanian origin, was born in Philadelphia. She worked in a clothing factory until her children were born. She spoke in English with her children, and in Yiddish with her parents.

Lipman's earliest memories are of the dreams he had before he was two years old in which he could fly, and accounts of a history of tedious and boring schooling, with the exception of some English literature classes, and the lessons he learned in Hebrew School, which allowed him to read the Torah out loud and to complete his bar mitzvah. He was nineteen years old when he first encountered the word *philosophy*. A career test suggested he should study engineering, which he could not afford. When he was twenty years old Lipman tried to volunteer for the air force during World War II, but was rejected due to his poor eyesight; he then joined the army. In the army he was able to access the university experience which his financial situation had barred him from. He studied two semesters at Stanford University in California and, once the war was finished, he continued studying for two more years in one of the two US universities created in Europe—Shrivenham, near London. At that time he had already read an anthology of John Dewey and the *Ethics* of Spinoza. He took his first course in philosophy when he was twenty-two years old, and this inspired him to visit David Hume's house in Scotland where he felt intensely "at home" in philosophy. By the end of the war Lipman had earned two medals—which he did not especially value—and the opportunity to study for four years as a doctorate student at the institution he had so much wanted to attend: Columbia University in New York. During these years he met his main intellectual influence, John Dewey, when Dewey was already retired from his academic activities. Lipman was mentored in his doctorate by Meyer Shapiro, and after a frustrating defense of his dissertation (afterword published as *What Happens in Art?*) in which for the first time he experienced some of the miseries of academic life, he was awarded a Fulbright Scholarship to conduct research for two years in Europe. During his time in Europe he met the African-American Wynona Moore, with whom he shared philosophical and political impulses, and whom he would marry in 1952 in Paris. The couple remained married for twenty-two years. Wynona was part of the liberal base of the Democratic Party and beginning in 1970, served for thirty years as a Senator of the State of New Jersey.

Upon returning to the United States, Lipman took a position as a Professor within the Faculty of Pharmacy at the University of Columbia. During the 1950s he met Justus Buchler, his most prominent influence together with Dewey. Lipman's two children were born: Karen in 1959 and Will in 1960, and Lipman and his family moved to the small city of Montclair, in the State of New Jersey, very close to New York where he continued to work. A more profound interest in education and childhood emerged during this time. This interest was not so much a result of his experiences with his two children as of a reading of Hannah Arendt's article, "Reflections on Little Rock," in *Dissent*, 1959. For Lipman, Arendt's arguments were tremendously conservative in terms of their favoring a family's control rather than society's control of education, and because he understood her as placing national interests over the social rights of African Americans.

Soon after reading Arendt' article, Lipman began to re-think his own education, and to consider the need for a radical change in his life. The organization of a successful art exposition in New York, overcoming various new challenges, entering into new worlds and experiences and emerging fuller from them, helped Lipman gain self-confidence. Education also became the defining challenge of his life. Reading about the experience of *Summerhill* did not deeply impress Lipman as much as an exposition of art by children studying there did. Lipman began to speculate on children's capacity not only to feel deeply but also to think deeply. The student protests in various universities during 1968 convinced him of the need for an urgent reform, both practical and theoretical, within all levels of the educational system. In spite of being sympathetic with some of the students' grievances—such as giving students more participation in governing the universities—he believed that these movements would lead not to the transformation of the universities but to their destruction. He also believed that educational remediation was needed at the base of the system. Lipman held a position similar to the one held by Plato in the first books of *The Republic*.

The need to write a philosophical story, one which could be read by both children and adults, began to become increasingly clear. In 1967 Lipman wrote *Harry Stottlemier's Discovery*, which has now been translated into more than forty languages. During the writing of *Harry* he progressively felt himself becoming a creator, an innovator, even surpassing John Dewey whom he critiqued for never having written a curriculum taking scientific inquiry as its model. *Harry Stottlemier's Discovery* was for Lipman a real introduction to philosophy, both for children and for their teachers. Each chapter is developed to a particular branch of philosophy, such as education, arts, religion, and constitutes a specific "philosophy of." It is not a book meant to be about philosophy, but rather philosophy itself vividly recreated in the lives of the reading children and teachers. In 1969 the first edition of *Harry* was printed and in 1970 Lipman, with two assistants, coordinated the first philosophical experiences with the book in a Public School of Montclair. The experiences, which took place over nine weeks, and which consisted of two weekly sessions each lasting forty minutes, demonstrated promising results in terms of the logical reasoning of the students who, according to Dr. Milton Bierman of the Montclair Board of Education improved their logical reasoning "by 27 months of mental age."

Lipman eventually moved from Columbia to Montclair State University where he found better institutional conditions to cultivate his project.

There he met Ann Margaret Sharp, with whom he would work together in seeking acknowledgment from the philosophical academy, and for funds to develop his idea and bring it to schools. In 1975 Lipman and Sharp conducted their first training workshop in p4c and it became clear that greater energy and work had to be devoted to teacher education in order to make the program work. Lipman begin to work with his team on a manual for *Harry* which could be used by teachers with no philosophical background, and to write the other novels that would complete the p4c program. Intensive seminars were offered, first at Rutgers and then in Mendham. Various positive reviews by the media and a film produced by the BBC resulted in greater exposure to the project, first in the United States and then in the rest of the world. People from all continents became interested in *Philosophy for Children* and with the invaluable help of Ann Sharp the dissemination of the program to other countries had begun.

Lipman's life is full of narratives of unexpected adventures in places as far ranging as Nigeria and Mexico. His autobiography offers details on meetings with prominent figures as various as Paulo Freire and Taraq Aziz. He documents unexpected accomplishments, such as being named Honorary Scholar of Montclair State University, and the offer to have his records kept at the Library of Living Philosophers at the Carbondale Campus of University of Southern Illinois together with the works of Dewey and other pragmatists. In his autobiography, Lipman also relates his encounters with organizations such as APA and UNESCO. We also learn that Lipman lived through extreme personal setbacks: the death of his son Will due to lymphoma when he was only twenty-four years old, his own battle with Parkinson's, and the unexpected death of his second wife Teri—thirty years younger, a Christian mystic, the result of an unexplained problem with a prescription medicine. Recently, Ann Margaret Sharp's passing must have caused him great pain. Within the same year that his philosophical companion died, Lipman himself has now passed away, in the Green Hill Retirement Community in West Orange, New Jersey, maybe a little more alone than he deserved to be after having given so much to so many.

Matthew Lipman has passed away. A philosopher and educator committed and coherent in seeing his ideas through to their last consequence, someone determined to "do something" in this unjust world. This something was nothing less than the completion of a curriculum which makes the practice of philosophy an educational reality for children from the moment they enter school. He also left behind a prominent theoretical body of work that supports his program and presents his perspectives on education.

In the last pages of his autobiography, Lipman (2008) asks himself whether his efforts to reform education have been successful. He affirms without doubt that the Philosophy for Children enterprise has made a lasting impact on the education system. Lipman maintained that once installed in the elementary school curriculum, philosophy would thrive for a long time, because even though there might be other ways of practicing philosophy and other philosophical perspectives might appear, no other discipline could do what philosophy as a discipline does: help children think critically, creatively, and with empathy about themselves and the world in which they live. This is Matthew Lipman's legacy, and the legacy of his foundation. Both remain firm and open at the same time, and they widely exceed the specific program he built and defended in order to see philosophy practiced in schools.

More than anything a kind and honorable person has died, a good person, someone with integrity. I had the pleasure and honor to experience the enormous personal and intellectual generosity of which Lipman was capable. I first met him in 1993 in one of the workshops that he conducted for years in Mendham, New Jersey. Shortly after meeting him, I became his assistant, and he guided me in the writing of my PhD thesis. This was in fact his first experience as a doctoral mentor. He could not have been more open and collaborative in the process. My commitment and enthusiasm for his ideas are continuously growing, but at the same time, in more recent years I have felt a need to recreate his ideas based on other methodological, theoretical, and practical beliefs. I have been engaged in this work for the past fifteen years.

Matthew Lipman, the creator of Philosophy for Children, has gone. Certainly, a number of deserved homages will take place in many parts of the world. His body of work will continue to be studied, practiced, and published throughout the world. And, perhaps what for Mat would probably be most important, thousands and thousands of children will continue to read his novels in the most diverse languages, and teachers will continue to consult his manuals looking for meaning in their educational practice. Both the novels and manuals will continue to establish a place for the most diverse philosophical inquiries to occur.

Matthew Lipman has passed on, and with him, an important piece of the educational relationship between childhood and philosophy. Just as his colleagues and friends are sad, childhood and philosophy are sad too.

But childhood and philosophy also rejoice, as do those who, through Lipman, came to see childhood and philosophy in a different way. The moment he entered the realms of childhood and philosophy as well as our lives nothing could continue being as it was. Everything has become, in a sense, more childlike, and, in another sense, more philosophical. Everything has turned out to be more childishly philosophical, or philosophically childish. Everything thanks to Matthew Lipman. Thank you so much for all, Mat. (PS: As a good-bye present to your uniqueness, I offer you, Mat, this story. I believe you will like it because it reveals childhood as a force of uniqueness in the world.):

> One time, investigating in the backyard of our house in Temuco the tiny objects and minuscule beings of my world, I came upon a hole in one of the boards of the fence. I looked through the hole and saw a landscape like that behind our house, uncared for, and wild. I moved back a few steps, because I sensed vaguely that something was about to happen. All of a sudden a hand appeared, a tiny hand of a boy about my own age. By the time I came close again, the hand was gone, and in its place there was a marvelous white sheep. The sheep's wool was faded. Its wheels had escaped. All of this only made it more authentic. I had never seen such a wonderful sheep. I looked back through the hole but the boy had disappeared. I went into the house and brought out a treasure of my own: a pinecone, opened, full of odor and resin, which I adored. I set it down in the same spot and went off with the sheep. I never saw either the hand or the boy again. And I have never again seen a sheep like that either. The toy I lost finally in a fire. But even now, in 1954, almost fifty years old, whenever I pass a toy shop, I look furtively into the window, but it's no use. They don't make sheep like that anymore. (Neruda, 1974: 7; our translation)

4
The Politics of Formation: A Critique of Philosophy for Children

Abstract: *This chapter offers a more educational and political critique of p4c, centered on a critique of the idea of formation. Starting from Plato's idea of the relationships among childhood, education, and politics, it shows the birth of a continuous line of thought and practice, in which p4c surprisingly establishes itself.*

Keywords: critique of Philosophy for Children; formation; Gilles Deleuze; Plato; Socrates; what does it mean to think?

Kohan, Walter Omar. *Philosophy and Childhood: Critical Perspectives and Affirmative Practices.* New York: Palgrave Macmillan, 2014. DOI: 10.1057/9781137469175.0008.

Philosophy for Children is an enterprise, now more than forty years old, which usually presents itself as "education for democracy" or "education for (better) thinking." In this chapter, I'll raise a number of questions about some basic assumptions of the enterprise. I would like to clarify that I am speaking from within the context of Latin America—Brazil in particular—where p4c is certainly popular, probably as much as in those parts of the world where it is most popular. The numbers are quite impressive: since 1985, thousands of teachers have been in touch with some kind of formation through the centers of p4c. Through the program, hundreds of thousands of children have had some contact with philosophy.

At the same time, there are other signs, apart from those in educational institutions, that feed optimism concerning the social function of philosophy: movements that attempt to take philosophy to the city, philosophical cafes, cyber-philosophy, philosophical counseling, philosophy for the elderly. These signs apparently indicate that philosophy occupies quite a different position in Brazilian culture than it did some decades ago, during the past dictatorship, when it was not feasible in higher education, a recluse in a few high schools, unthinkable in elementary school, and impracticable in the public space of the city. In the face of this new data, many lovers of philosophy are happy. People even speak about a philosophy fever, an explosion of philosophy in Brazil.

I am somewhat more cautious. I don't consider it interesting that philosophy just occupies public spaces. What matters fundamentally is to understand the function which philosophy is developing, both inside and out of schools—the type of philosophy that is practiced (and taught), its relationships with other areas of knowledge, with the institution of school, and with other economic, social, and political institutions of the time. And it is especially important to consider the kind of relationship that teachers and students involved with philosophy establish to the discipline and to each other. What matters more than anything else is the kind of thinking that is affirmed and is promoted under the name of philosophy. I would like to reflect on this particular question in this chapter.

When the increased public presence of philosophy is seen from the perspective of these larger, broader issues, optimism decreases or, at best, changes. One form of optimism leaves and another enters. Michel Foucault makes an interesting distinction between two types of optimism. In an interview conducted some years before his death, the interviewer questioned him concerning the usual imputation of pessimist that he carried. In response, Foucault proposed two forms of optimism.

The first is that of someone who thinks that "anyway, things are splendid, this could not be better" (Foucault, 1994b: 182). This optimism is of little interest, naive, conformist, in France, in Brazil, in the USA, and in any other place. But there is a second form of optimism, which is more interesting. It is that of one who says: "so many things could be changed, fragile as they are, linked more to contingencies than to needs, more to the arbitrary than to the ineluctable, more to complex historical but passing contingencies than to inevitable anthropological constants" (ibid.). If the first form of optimism is conniving with and legitimating the state of things, the second opens a space for transformation. To notice that things could always be otherwise is a start to transforming them.

It would be of no little interest if lovers of philosophy—in Brazil and perhaps in other places—were optimistic in this second sense, if it were noticeable that the attitude toward philosophy in educational institutions was neither conformist nor complacent. It would indeed be significant if we noticed how much philosophical teaching—which is the very practice of philosophy itself—needs philosophical questioning, how important it is for the teaching of philosophy that teachers and students establish a philosophical relationship with their practice, by which I mean a fully open, critical and questioning one.

The situation of philosophy in educational institutions is very complex. I do not intend to offer a total or comprehensive view of that situation, not even in Brazil; such a vision—which, besides excessively pretentious, I have no conditions to offer—would be an oversimplification. Rather, I would like to propose some perspectival questions born out of my particular reality. I am thinking of the term "perspective" in the Nietzschean sense—where, for instance, in the *Genealogy of the Morals* (3, §12), F. Nietzsche affirms that to look is always to look *at* something, and that there can only be a perspectival look—there is no unique, global look. Nietzsche also affirms that the more different pairs of eyes could look at the same thing, the more complete would be our concept of it. My own perspective is based in the last more than twenty years of intense commitment to philosophical inquiry with children, mostly in Argentina and Brazil.

I realize that this perspective could be made more complex, richer, and less simplistic, and as such, I count on the reader's contribution—each reader's pair of eyes. In philosophy nobody looks in the place of another, no one can think in the space of the other. Either each one uses his or her own eyes, or else another looks through them. In that case, properly speaking, he or she would not be seeing anything, just lending his or her eyes to another. Each one thinks for himself or herself or else there is another one thinking for him or her. In that case, he or she would not be really thinking, just lending his or her mind to another. I intend neither to look for you nor to think for you; I just wish to share with the reader a suspicion that might help us to think about the teaching of philosophy and our relationship with it. In this sense it can help us to think for ourselves and on ourselves.

My perspectival suspicion is that p4c is not as transformative, as revolutionary, and as radical, as it is desirable for it to be to make any difference in these neo-capitalistic, global times—not, at least, in the usual form its educational theory and practice takes. In other words, it is not as actually transformative as it is potentially so. I am basing these statements on two points: the meaning which p4c gives to philosophy in its relationship to education and childhood, and the way it answers the question "what does it mean to think?" as it is applied to philosophical practice among teachers and children. Certain limits implicit in the educational and political agenda of p4c will be exposed after an analysis of these basic issues. I am not trying to suggest that we should abandon p4c. Quite the contrary. We should deepen it through reconstructing it on other bases and through other practices.

The argument which follows is composed of five sections. The first four will explore the relationship between four major concepts: education, philosophy, childhood, and thinking. I will put into question the common assumption that different philosophical movements—such as p4c—have shared about philosophical education: the idea that the teaching of philosophy should serve the formation of an ideal person or an ideal society; in other words, the idea that philosophy contributes to a formative *paideia*. I will specify in what sense Western education, at least from Plato's *Republic* on, has almost always been associated with the idea of formation. In the second section, I will give some examples of how philosophy has been involved with this formative education. In the third section, I will consider the concept of childhood that sustains the pedagogies and philosophies of formation. In the fourth section, I will question what the French philosopher Gilles Deleuze has called "a moralistic or dogmatic image of thinking" (2003: 129 ss.) that, far from helping us teach for better thinking, yet disables us to think philosophically. In the last section, I will sketch some proposals which locate the experience of thinking and philosophy in the context of a non-formative educational logic. My aim is to open some paths of inquiry, and to propose some basic elements which might contribute to the reconstruction of the idea of doing philosophy with children.

4.1   Education in the service of formation

In Book II of the *Republic*, Plato discusses how the guardians of the *pólis* should be educated in order to guarantee a fair community. The examination of the question will enable us to determine, Socrates says, the genesis—the starting point, or cause—of justice and injustice in Athens at the time (II, 376d). That examination locates the cause of injustice in the classic texts (Homer and Hesiod) that sustain traditional education in Greece, texts that affirm, according to Plato, values contrary to those that should be practiced in the *pólis*. If we want a just society, Socrates argues, we must change the texts by which the Athenians are educated. When discussing which stories should be substituted for the traditional ones, Socrates has the following dialogue with Adimantus:[1]

> What is this education to be, then? Perhaps we shall hardly invent a system better than the one which long experience has worked out, with its two branches for the cultivation of the mind and of the body. And I suppose we shall begin with the mind, before we start physical training.
> Naturally.
> Under that head will come stories. [...] And the beginning, as you know, is always the most important part, specially in dealing with anything young and tender. That is the time when the character is being moulded and easily takes any impress one may wish to stamp on it. (II, 376e–377b)

The first years of life are the most important, says Socrates. For that reason, he affirms, children will not be allowed to listen to stories that contain lies and attitudes contrary to those expected from them in the future. Because if we think of life as a sequence of development, as a progressive coming-into-being, as a fruit that will be born of planted seeds, all that comes later will depend on those first steps. This is what makes these first moments extraordinarily important, because of the indelible marks that are received in the early years (378e). For that reason, special care will be taken during those first stages, not so much for what children are but for what they will become, for what they will generate at a later time. In the end, these small creatures will be the future guardians, rulers of the *pólis*. Therefore in designing their education, what should be mainly considered is what they can be and what they ought to be,

Plato suggests. The new ones are what their elders want them to be. In the case of Plato, the children with the best natures ought to be, in the future, philosophical kings, philosophers ruling, in a just manner, the dreamed-of *pólis*.

In this text of the *Republic*, it is someone external—the educator, the philosopher, the politician, the legislator, the founder of the *pólis*—who will think and plant in each child the seed of what he or she should be in the future. Implicit here is the idea of education as giving form to another. To give someone a form. To inform him or her. Which form? In the case of Plato it is the form of the Forms: the Ideas, those *a priori* models, paradigms, each transcendent *eidos*—which will indicate the norms for the formation of the young. Formed in this way, children will be able to be the kind of citizens necessary for a just state, and will facilitate the worldly empire of truth, goodness, and beauty.

In this paradigm, children are not so much important for being children but for being future adults. The founders of the *pólis*, who know the risks involved in growth, want the best for them—what they consider the best, but in fact is the best thing for they *themselves*, what they have not been able to be but think others ought to be. Through the education of the newcomers, adults will have the *pólis* they have not been able to build through their own education. Certainly, they will accompany the new ones, help them, show their "best intentions." They will undergo all sorts of sacrifices to make this utopia possible. It is in this political formation that Western education has traditionally found its meaning: to accompany the new (*hoi neoi*) in the passage from an old to a new world—new for the old, old for the new ones—that the olders will build with the help of the new; or the new will bring with the help of the olders, as you prefer.

Two basic elements characterize this "formative" *paideia* (Larrosa, 1996: 21): (a) children are educated to develop certain dispositions that, it is considered, exist in them roughly or potentially; (b) they are educated to form—to give form to—a prescriptive model that has been established apart from them. In this approach, education is understood as a moral task (Larrosa, 1996: 423), as normative, as adjusting what is to what ought to be. According to this orientation, our ideals will channel the development of an educational practice. Children represent adults' opportunity to carry out their ideals, and education is an appropriate tool for such an end. Formative education doesn't resist the temptation to appropriate the novelty of the new, to make an eminently political task out of education, and to make of a given politics the final significance of the educational enterprise (Arendt, 1961: 176).

4.2 Philosophy in the service of formation and politics

In the *Republic* not only education but also philosophy is in the service of formation and of politics. On the one hand, philosophy forms those who enter in contact with its knowledge. It is philosophical knowledge that, according to Plato, will make of the best natures the best rulers. For that reason, when Socrates discusses with Plato's brothers who will be chosen to participate in the highest studies, he offers the condition that they should be lovers of philosophy, because such are those of the most rigorous character (VI, 503b). In this sense, philosophy as knowledge will facilitate good formation, the best destination in those best of natures. This is also the sense in which Plato's *Republic* proposes an aristocratic (*aristós*, best) *pólis*.

On the other hand, philosophy is pedagogic because these keepers of philosophy, the ones who contain its knowledge, who know the Forms, will educate all the others according to the knowledge in which they have been formed. It is not an option: they will be forced to it (VII, 519b). Glauco asks Socrates about the fairness of such an obligation:

> Shall we not be doing them an injustice, if we force on them a worse life than they *might* have?
> You have forgotten again, my friend, that the law is not concerned to make any one class specially happy, but to ensure the welfare of the commonwealth as a whole. By persuasion or constraint it will unite the citizens in harmony, making them share whatever benefits each class can contribute to the common good; and its purpose in forming men of that spirit was not that each should be left to go his own way, but that they should be instrumental in binding the community into one. (VII, 519e–520a)

Duty of state. The whole is more important than the part. The unity and good health of the state must be preserved before anything else. These natures—the best by virtue of their natural dispositions and the philosophical knowledge they have acquired—should be sacrificed in favor of the common good. After all, the state has formed them to govern the others. The rulers ought to philosophize and the philosophers ought to govern, so that the *pólis* be more rational, more just, more harmonious, and more beautiful. They have no option. Thus philosophy becomes an eminently political task, and politics acquires its form philosophical knowledge. Some apply their philosophical knowledge to politicize the new, to make them participants of a *pólis* already defined for them. Instituted politics is a way of extending philosophical knowledge to the whole community.

From my perspective, most Western conceptions of the educational dimension of philosophy—including p4c—have this characteristic, beyond all its differences in the details. Admittedly, aristocracy has given place to democracy. There are no longer transcendental Forms. No more philosopher kings. But are there any significant differences from the *Republic* in the structural relationship affirmed between education, philosophy, and politics?

Let's examine, for example, the way in which Matthew Lipman has recently justified the introduction of philosophy into schools. According to Lipman, to bring philosophy to children is justified because it offers them at least three tools that all participants in a democracy need: (1) a rich and varied treatment of universal and controversial concepts such as truth, justice, and freedom; (2) an education in thinking that leads them to be higher-order thinkers (which includes critical, creative, and caring thinking); (3) an opportunity for significant dialogue that fosters their better judgment (1998: 6–7). According to Lipman, the logic of democracy (*one* democracy, understood as deliberative inquiry) determines the purposes of teaching philosophy. To bring philosophy to children with its history, its methods, and its themes is justified for the social advantages that such a practice will create (Lipman, 1998: 198). If a more solid democracy is desired outside schools, democratic practices must be brought into them; philosophy is so important for what children will be, in order to make them tolerant, responsible, pluralistic citizens. In this way, a "well-understood" democracy is normative of the practice of philosophy.

Although there are enormous differences between Plato's and Lipman's concepts of education, politics, and philosophy, I also see a remarkable similarity in the way both connect them: the educational potential of philosophy is justified because of its political force to open space for a given utopia; the inclusion of philosophy in education—of the young in the case of Lipman, of adults in Plato—is defended on the basis of its formative political potential to lead to a better world. Whatever the differences in their specific agendas, both philosophers of education consider that the practice of philosophy includes a basic political component, and both see philosophy as an educational vehicle for that component. While affirming different social orders and dissimilar concepts of citizenship, education, and philosophy, both consider children, before anything else, to be future citizens of a desired political order.

4.3 About education and childhood

The essence of education resides in natality—in the fact that human beings are born into the world (Arendt, 1961: 174). The world and those recently arrived in it are mutually strange; there is no continuity among them, but rupture. With every beginning life, a new beginning is born, a new being that is actualized in each action and in each word (Masschelein, 1990: 768). The new being, the child, the *in-fans*, with no voice, speaks from its own birth; with its birth it arouses a doubt, puts us in question, breaks a given order, a certain state of things.

Education, then, might be seen as a reaction to the experience of birth (Masschelein, 1990: 769), to the unexpected and unpredictable irruption of another being—someone new arrives in a world that, from its perspective, is also new. Understood in this sense, education is possible only because of an inexhaustible plurality. Without plurality there is no education. Education comes into being when someone else, someone "other"—"an-other"—is born and this birth has to be responded in some way.

Does the fact that education is a reaction to plurality imply that all education needs to be conservative? The history of education and of the educational presence of philosophy in the West would seem to respond affirmatively. Let's go back to Plato. The *Republic* critiques the traditional education of the Athenians, and proposes, in some respects, a kind of state radically different from the imperialistic, slave-holding, male-dominated Athenian one: no empire, no slaves, women under the same conditions of men and eligible to rule the *pólis*. Nevertheless, in its educational program, the *Republic* is tremendously reactionary in the face of the novelty of the newcomers: in fact this novelty is not acknowledged, considered, or even perceived. Faced with the novelty of the newcomers, one single, total, comprehensive model is imposed. The "new" model is new for the Greek tradition, but old for those who arrive into the world. Philosophy, as we have previously seen, understood as philosophical knowledge, is a good tool for eradicating their novelty for the purposes of the state. In this way, philosophy, turned official—made pedagogy of a desired order—loses its subversive, much less its transformative powers.

4.4 Philosophy as experience of thinking: critique of the dogmatic image of thought

What then should we educate for if not to develop the potential of the new and to form citizens for a better world? How can we think the purposes of educational philosophy—or philosophical education—if not as in the service of political formation? These questions are closely connected to the way in which we think about the question "what is philosophy?" In this pursuit, the category of "experience" plays a major part, in that it overcomes the classic dichotomies between philosophy and philosophizing, between professors of philosophy and philosophers, and between theory and practice. I consider that philosophy is an experience of thinking, and that teaching philosophy has to do with promoting such experiences.[2]

I am thinking of the term "experience" in the hermeneutical sense. As Gadamer has said, experience is an unsubstitutable component of human existence (p. 1999). It is something that no one living as an historical being can avoid, and something that no one can live for another. As beings, we are characterized by experience. Experiences can neither be transferred nor repeated. When we repeat an experience we turn it into an experiment, we kill its character as experience, we transform it into repetition of the same. In this sense, philosophy, as experience, is radically different from science, at least in the latter's more positivistic form. In science it is precisely the fact that any person can repeat experiences that sustains their validity. By contrast, philosophy as experience of thinking is unique, unrepeatable, and nonnegotiable. Philosophical thinking cannot be turned into scientific knowledge, cannot be normalized, uniformized, or standardized. In philosophy, no one can think for another.

But to say that philosophy is an experience of thinking is not enough. What form of thinking does the experience of philosophy affirm and promote? These questions lead us to analyze something that Deleuze called "the dogmatic or moralistic image of thought." This image is expressed in forms such as "everybody already knows that ...," "no one can deny that ...," "everyone recognizes that ...," forms that turn common sense into cognitive assumptions. It is specified in the following eight postulates (Deleuze, 2003/1997): (1) the postulate of the principle: it assumes the thinker's good will and the good nature of thought; (2) the postulate of common sense: common sense as *concordia facultatum*, and "good sense" as what guarantees this concord; (3) the postulate of the model, or of recognition: inviting all the faculties to exercise upon an object supposedly the same; (4) the postulate of the element or of representation that reduces difference to the dimensions of the Same and the Similar, the Analogous and the Opposite; (5) the postulate of the negative, in which error expresses anything negative in thinking as a product of external mechanisms; (6) the postulate of the proposition: designation is constituted as the space of truth; (7) the postulate of modality or solutions, which tends to define problems only in terms of the possibility of their being solved; (8) the postulate of the end: learning and culture are subordinated to knowledge and method.

These eight postulates describe the dogmatic image of thought. Let us analyze one of them. The postulate of the model, or of recognition, sets up a division between the empiric and the transcendental. It is presupposed that thought is by nature right, that it knows itself what it means to think; that it is itself a unity and always happens in reference to another unit—the subject—which embraces it together with the other faculties (perception, memory, imagination, understanding); and that thinking is guided by the reduction of difference to the same. But recognition, Deleuze says, cannot promote anything other than the recognized and the recognizable; it is unable to generate more than conformity to the same. Deleuze's purpose is not to deny that recognition has any role in human life or that it cannot contribute to the carrying out of vital functions. It can form the basis for many things, but not of thought—if thought has to do with difference, plurality, and diversity. In this sense, when we recognize, we do not really think. When a difference is recognized, it is appropriated—it stops being a difference. Thus at the base of the image of thought as recognition lies the own impossibility of thinking. And in the negation of that image lies its possibility. If philosophical thought has to do with actual thinking, it is because from it can emerge the new, the different, what today is not recognized nor recognizable, not even thinkable.

From whence can philosophical thought arise if not from recognition? From an encounter, Deleuze suggests. The results of any real encounter cannot be anticipated, foreseen, deduced. It is the encounter with what forces us to think, with what puts us in doubt, with what takes us out of our conformity, our normality, our natural attitude. In this sense, thinking is unpredictable; it is an event, it is the free operation of difference and complex repetition in the realm of the heterogeneous—an uncertain, accidental, unexpected encounter. This means that where there are predetermined forms, ideas, or models, philosophical thought will not find its place.

If the experience of thinking cannot be transmitted or anticipated, is it possible to teach it? How? What in fact is the relationship between teaching and learning? How is it possible to facilitate anyone's learning? Could the space be generated for someone to learn an experience (of thinking)? P4c proposes, among other things, a method for teaching how to think well. Is the "good" a category that helps us to think or that disables our thinking? Are there in fact methods for teaching how to think (well) at all?

4.5 Education, philosophy, thinking, childhood

To learn has to do with loving and dying. Therefore, to educate is an amorous act—for the encounters that it propitiates—and, at the same time, a murderous act—for the dying homogeneity, for the heterogeneity it welcomes, for the difference it needs in that space of encounter. To learn is to meet the other, in oneself, or oneself in the other, loving and dying. Therefore, the teacher who teaches by presenting a model to imitate really teaches nothing. He or she doesn't teach because there is no learning when there is reproduction of the same; he or she can even disturb someone's learning in this way, because to really learn does not mean to learn anything external, any knowledge previously given, it does not even mean "to build" a knowledge. To learn means to give space to difference in one's thinking.

Is it possible to teach to think? How? Since most of us are teachers, how do we make possible others' learning? How do we create conditions for anyone to learn anything? And since we are concerned with teaching philosophy, how do we generate the space for someone to learn to think philosophically? Any answer to these questions has its limits, as a thinking experience. We can never know ahead of time if someone will learn something, much less by which roads he or she might achieve that learning. The difficulties multiply when it concerns learning to think. But we know that without the experience of the heterogeneous there is no learning, no thinking. It is not possible to learn to think without thinking, without loving and dying.

In my view, there are at least two crucial issues which any proposal for "teaching to think" should consider, if it is really interested in philosophical thought. First, no entrainment between teaching and learning should be assumed. The assumption that teaching always implies learning, and that learning always implies teaching, does not facilitate the path to thinking. In other words, we cannot be sure that if when someone teaches another learns, and that if someone learns it is because another taught her.

Second, to understand philosophical thought as set of abilities or tools condemns it to the mirrored repetition of the same—if not of the same content, at least of the same model of thinking. Philosophical thought is not an ability, but an event; not a tool, but an experience. As ability or tool, it is mechanized, technicized. Philosophical thought, thinking philosophically, cannot be trained, but it can be prepared, expected, stimulated. We do not defend a romantic perspective or an obscure pedagogy. We are trying to think a philosophical pedagogy for teaching philosophy.

Nobody can think alone. We think with others. The question "is it at all possible to teach to think?" should be neither avoided nor undervalued by any teacher interested in teaching others to think philosophically. We don't know if it is possible to teach to think. We suspect that, if thinking is an encounter, teaching to think has to do with propitiating those encounters. But there are no formulas or prescriptions. No one learns what another teaches him or her when he or she really learns anything. At most there is an extensive and difficult preparation, through experience, promoting actual experiences of philosophical thinking. To learn to think (philosophically) means to find one's own road in thinking (philosophically) through difference, and no one can pass this on to anyone.

In order to teach to think (philosophically) it is necessary to learn to think (philosophically). We learn to think (philosophically) with, not from, others. Therefore, a nice image that a teacher can offer is of one who thinks with others—no matter what her age, race, or gender might be; who stages and promotes and facilitates experiences of thinking; who has no models and promotes no models; who offers others something to think about; who doesn't obstruct the road of his or her students; who propitiates encounters that she cannot herself advance or foresee.

In previous sections of this chapter, I have tried to show how education and philosophy have dominantly reacted to plurality. They have been guided by the ruling idea of education as political formation. In the West, we have mostly educated in order to form people, to "make something" of someone, to develop his or her thinking, his or her possibilities according to our "ought to be"—and philosophy, unthinkingly, has offered itself as a candidate for a role in this project of domination. As we have seen, this strategy presupposes a concept of childhood which emphasizes malleability, the absence of form, and the consequent necessity of being in-formed. It also affirms a dogmatic image of thought that hides an absence of philosophical thinking-as-experience that opens a space for difference. Let me propose some alternative points of view.

It seems to me that philosophy needs to liberate itself from any external determinant norm. When philosophy is practiced to affirm a politics—or a morality, a pedagogy, a religion, or any other determinant order—it is disabled. Morals, pedagogy, politics, and religion are problems for philosophy, not arrival points. When philosophy is the official voice of a politics or a morality—whether aristocratic or democratic, liberal or authoritarian—it loses its subversive and transformative power. Moreover, when any morality, politics, or religion is set up as a purpose of philosophy, philosophy itself becomes impossible. If philosophy is possible at all, it is because morality, politics, religion constitute an empty space, an interrogation, an interval.

As an experience of thinking, philosophy doesn't admit of any definitive order. It aspires to think the unthinkable. It suspects that the impossible is possible. It testifies to the sovereignty of the question. It affirms plurality, other orders; it shows its other possibilities, its aporias, its confrontations, its exclusions, its emergences-into-being. It opens the doors to difference. In short, it allows an encounter with childhood.

What might this experience of philosophy look like in the classroom, in the café, on the street? Socrates is always an inspirational source for philosophy, because he is a founder, and because he left the city with the doors open; also, for what he said and what has been said of him, for not having written anything and for having taught others to write, for teaching philosophy through philosophy; for the experiences of philosophical thinking that he seemed to have made possible in the city. He suggests a path for us: to put into question the relationships between education, philosophy, and politics. He is an image, an example—not a model—of the subversive, non-official voice of philosophy, of the educational possibilities of philosophy in its relationship to politics, an affirmation of a philosophical experience of politics. Through the exercise of philosophy, Socrates opposes himself to the diverse positive political regimes he experiences—to democracies, oligarchies and tyrannies—nor does he affirms any positive political order. He questions the politics affirmed in Athens. He resists it. He interrogates it. He unmasks it.

Socrates has no political project for which to educate, and at the same time, he is one of the few, if not the only, Athenians who, according to Plato, is devoted to the "true art of politics" (*Gorgias* 521d)—the only one who practices the true politics of his time. Significantly for philosophy, for that reason he is condemned to death by the instituted politicians. Socrates makes of philosophy an eminently political task, and of the exercise of politics a form of philosophy with a radically different sense from the one proposed by Plato: the experience of philosophy finds its place in a form of life sustained through questioning, in the *a-poria*, the absence of *poros*, or end. Philosophy needs to think philosophically its political and pedagogical dimensions. Socrates—the less Platonic one, the Socrates of the early dialogues—might help us to think these dimensions as non-formative, in the sense I have given the term in this chapter.

After Socrates, among Plato and his followers, the philosophical question turned into the philosophical answer, resistance turned into proposition, and the unhidden was made absolute reality. Plato understood the politics of philosophy as a statement of utopia, of a common norm, that just *pólis*, where each part plays its corresponding function (*Republic* IV 432). In this way philosophy alienated itself in utopia, in a politics, in the postulation of a norm, in a prescriptive way immune to philosophical questioning. Its pedagogy could not avoid reflecting this state, and philosophy continued to be taught in a non-philosophical sense. If the teaching of philosophy wishes to liberate itself from this dogmatic mask, it needs to divest itself of its Platonism, to refuse its non-philosophical preoccupation with political and pedagogical formation.

Is the experience of philosophy possible in an institution, such as the school, which is overwhelmed by a determinative order? Is a philosophical education through philosophy possible? Is an encounter between philosophy and childhood possible? These questions are immense, endless, but,

> *If we don't expect the unexpected we won't find it, since it is not findable and is very difficult of access.* (Heraclitus, fragment 18)

Faced with such immense questions, it might be interesting to listen to a philosophical child such as Heraclitus. And, while thinking with him, we might still finish with such sort of childish questions.

Notes

1 Quotations of Plato's *Republic* are taken from Francis M. Cornford's translation at the Oxford University Press (1971).
2 I have explored this assumption in Kohan, Walter, Leal, Bernardina, Teixeira, Álvaro (orgs.), 2000.

Part II
Philosophy in Children: Affirmative Practices

5
Philosophy at Public Schools of Brasilia, DF

Abstract: *This chapter describes a project of practicing Philosophy with Children in public schools of the Federal District of Brazil. It covers the theoretical, methodological, and practical dimensions of this project and evaluates it as a teacher education proposal.*

Keywords: childhood; philosophical inquiry; Philosophy in School; Philosophy with Children; Public Schooling; Teacher Education

Kohan, Walter Omar. *Philosophy and Childhood: Critical Perspectives and Affirmative Practices.* New York: Palgrave Macmillan, 2014. DOI: 10.1057/9781137469175.0010.

The following narrative offers a vision of a project that took place between 1997 and 2002 at the University of Brasilia and some Public Schools of the Federal District of Brazil, involving both teachers and students of these institutions.

5.1   A little of history

P4c arrived in Brazil through Catherine Young Silva (US American naturalized Brazilian, 1937–1993). Catherine had her Master's in p4c at Montclair State University, New Jersey, USA and, returned to Brazil to take care of translating and adapting Lipman's program and familiarizing his proposal, training teachers and developing its practice in schools. In January 1985, with a group of colleagues—among them were Marcos Lorieri and Ana Luiza Falcone—she created the now defunct Brazilian Center of p4c (CBFC). With her natural charisma, Catherine invited colleagues and younger professors and formed new generations of teachers and monitors that disseminated this proposal among Brazil during the past twelve years. The work went on conquering teachers and schools, expanding all through the country. Today, several groups work in p4c, both with Lipman and alternative materials.

In Brasilia, dissemination of p4c began in 1992. The pioneer was Ana Míriam Wuensch who constituted a Nucleus in 1993 at a private net of schools. Like Catherine in São Paulo, Ana Míriam took care of the teacher's formation, accompanied their practice in classroom, and worked toward the spreading of p4c in the Federal District. She was also responsible to sensitize academic philosophers and educators about the possibilities that bringing together philosophy and children could offer. It must be clarified that in Brasilia, philosophy, as a compulsory discipline at high school, came back to the curriculum during the 1980s after more than one decade of absence during military governments.

Philosophy being developed basically at elementary schools of the private system, at my arrival to Brasilia in 1997 as a visiting professor in the Department of Theory and Foundations of Education, I co-organized together with Ana Míriam a strategy to sensitize educational authorities and teachers about the possibilities philosophy could offer to basic education at the public school system. With the help of the Secretary of Education a number of events, including a dozen of awareness sessions, were organized between 1996 and 1997 involving around 500 teachers.

At the University of Brasilia a forum of professors of philosophy at high school was created with over fifty professors attending the workshop, courses, and Encounters. By December 1997, administrators of the Federal University, Secretary of Education, and a number of principals and teachers of public schools were ready to impulse and support a systematic project, named *Philosophy in School*, to develop the practice of philosophy at pre- and elementary public schools.

Curiously, at that time much more schools and teachers were interested in being part of the project that could be initially attended. Given that our material and human resources were very limited, a pilot experience was planned in four schools. So, the first task was to define criteria that would establish which schools to be let out of the nearly twenty interested that would take part in the first phase of the project. Some criteria were established with the local Secretary of Education: (a) how many teachers had taken part in the initial activities and were interested in developing the experience in each school; (b) an analysis of the justifications offered by these teachers to take part in the project; (c) the readiness of the school to commit itself to support the program giving a minimum of conditions to teachers and monitors to develop specific activities; (d) the geographical location of the school (looking for schools of places geographically differentiated inside the Federal District); (e) the socioeconomic level of reference of teachers and children (trying to reach different economic and social levels, from low class to middle class).

Finally, the following schools were invited to participate in the first stage of the project:

- CAIC Anísio Teixeira (Ceilândia, DF).
- Centro de Ensino AgroUrbano, (Núcleo Bandeirantes, DF).
- Escola Clase 03 (Gama, DF).
- Escola Clase 304 Norte (Asa Norte, DF).

Five teachers and pedagogical orientators of each school together with a total of eight BA students in Pedagogy, Philosophy, and Psychology took part of an intense weekly workshop celebrated at the University of Brasilia in February, 1998. Throughout the following five years I've directed the project till I moved to the State University of Rio de Janeiro in 2002. In these five years, a number of other schools entered the project. Participation was always volunteered and free: anyone could leave it whenever they had good reasons for it.

5.2 Main characteristics of *Philosophy in School*

The project was an extensional one in the sense that it placed academic research within society, seeking to contribute—through a dynamic and reciprocal process of teaching and learning—to the improvement of the thinking of teachers and children through philosophy. In a context where the dominant social pressures on the public school were faced around the need to "technologize" and "modernize" school, an alternative was proposed based on the practice of the philosophy, understood as the development of a cooperative thinking that questions the faiths, ideas, and values that underline the current social practices. In a society where the demands to "know more" were increasingly important and the ability to question was more and more considered a disturbance rather than a capacity, our proposal was based on problem-posed thinking rather than acquired knowledge or problem-solving thinking.

5.2.1 Strategies and methods: human resources

For pedagogic reasons, we considered that it is more convenient for children to practice philosophy with their own teachers—who share with them a number of hours a day—, than with "expert" philosophers who would meet them just for that practice. Regular teachers have better conditions to make philosophy just one more activity in school and to integrate its dispositions and methods among the rest of activities. In spite of the fact that educational institutions have not fostered but rather slumbered their philosophical sensibility, teachers interested in the practice of philosophy usually show a strong and "slept" disposition to the philosophical dimensions of their reality and a strong will to help children in identifying the problematic aspects of that same reality. One of our main tasks had been to strengthen those dispositions and help them to see philosophy as an active process in their practice rather than something ready that they should be prepared to learn and then "pass" onto children.

Philosophy in School pretended to be fully experimental, not only in its practice but also in the methods and texts it develops. We didn't pretend our teachers to "apply" a given method or program; we didn't think we should "train" them and "approve" or "allow" them to put a given program into practice. Rather, we supported their practice fostering together the main dispositions and attitudes of the act of philosophizing, as well as a methodology that could allow us to find together the best texts and activities to travel that same way of philosophizing with children. In this path, we tried to rescue the philosophical dimension and value of an enormously rich tradition of literature, music, art, and other cultural productions in Latin America grounded on a pedagogical practice that have many contributions to provide to philosophy.

Certainly, Matthew Lipman's approach, well-known elsewhere and named here as *p4c*, constituted for us an extraordinarily important point of reference in that it has been the most systematic and probably unique tentative to put together philosophy and children, and in that it had developed a number of practical experiences, in the whole world and particularly in Brazil, from which we had a lot to learn.

Nevertheless, any philosophical practice that prizes itself to be critical needs to find its own point of departure and its own way of philosophizing, inside a critical philosophy, sensitive to its context, there is no place for receipts, in the form of ready concepts, ideas, methods, texts, or values. A critical philosophy in practice needs to think—together, in cooperation and respect for differences—its own way to put its reality into question. Certainly, this task should not be developed out of nothing and with no method. We have a whole history of philosophy of at least twenty-five centuries in the West—and a younger but strong history of some decades of Philosophy with Children!—supporting our search and providing us with a whole set of options. But we cannot omit an educational practice that calls itself to be philosophical of the task of re-constructing and re-thinking its "how," its "what," its "whom," its "why," "its "for what." The philosophical dimension of this project demands us this philosophical inquiry about the disposition, textual and methodological possibilities of philosophy in its encounter with children.

In this collective work, the reality of each school and their children was our most important point of reference. Candanga schools at the Federal District of Brazil based their work on the methodology of "projects." Each month, the whole staff (principals, coordinators and teachers), according to its reality, needs and interests, planned their activities around a single theme—such as hygiene, rights, sexuality—that would give direction to the different disciplines and activities of the school all over that month. Each theme was developed in its different dimensions: mathematical, linguistic, historical, and so on. *Philosophy in Schools* tended to develop the practice of philosophy over these same themes to favor its potential aims and functions in, through, and among the other areas. Every month a different planning was being developed to explore that practice in each school. Besides, in a context where cultural compositions are highly intense in an oral dimension, but less importance is given to draw a written memory of those productions, the registration and evaluation of this experience of a vivid philosophy in elementary schools acquired specific and special significance.

This approach to the experience of philosophy has manifested itself, from our earliest experience of a first workshop, as a powerful source of an increasing questioning process directed to our own practice. There is no way to teach philosophy, but practicing it. Teachers and students have shown their potentiality as main actors of philosophical questioning. The following are samples of the questions that emerged from the beginning of that process:

- What conception of child and childhood is underlying this project and our philosophical practice with children?
- What conception of philosophy is underlying this project and our philosophical practice with children?
- Will this project help us to inquire new relationships between philosophy and education? How?
- How does this project dimensions/gives account of the difference proposed between philosophical contents and abilities?
- How should a teacher face her philosophical preparation/study to be able to improve on her practice of Philosophy with Children in the classroom?
- Which are the roles and contributions of the monitors to support teachers in their philosophical practice with children? How should monitors face their philosophical preparation/study to be able to improve their practice with teachers?
- What criteria should reach a text in order to be adequate to be used for philosophical practice with children? What rules or principles should guide the selection and creation of these texts?
- What are the main presuppositions and the basic procedures of a philosophical methodology in the education of children?
- When and how should we incorporate our philosophical practice into the other daily activities at school?
- How should we evaluate our work? Under which criteria? What instruments are appropriate for this task?

5.2.2 Aims and foundations

It can still be desirable to justify the meaning and sense of a project developing a practice of philosophy in public schools in the educational, economic, and social reality of a peripheral country such as Brazil. We could probably begin by appealing to the feelings that give root to philosophical questioning.

In effect, in these realities, philosophy usually nurtures from astonishment, dissatisfaction, ennui, surprise, and wonder. In a dominant injustice social world, where misery is a vivid dimension of the great majority of people's lives, these emotions are usually strong in our first years and less firm as they are confronted with diverse social strategies that tend to "naturalize" our life in society. In our experience of taking part in a diversity of institutions and practices, we are gradually less and less shocked and surprised by this dimension of the world; we are used to see it as something "natural," "ordinary," forgetting its extra-ordinary and social character. Foucault has clearly showed how the word "subject" illustrates this process:

> There are two meanings of the word *subject*: subject to someone else by control and dependence, and tied to his own identity by a conscience or self-knowledge. Both meanings suggest a form of power which subjugates and makes subject to. (M. Foucault, 1983: 212)

Socialization has directed to be a process that turns individuals into subjects. At present, the constitution of a subjectivity has do deal with a form of power that subjugates the individual to the normality and naturality of the current social order. Gradually we tend to pay less attention to the grounds and aims of social life and concentrate in the technical movements that presuppose those grounds and aims. In other words, we are moved to think about means and not about ends. The ends are shown to be natural, in the sense of being already established, determined, with no space for questioning. "That's the way it is" or "It has always been like this" are usual answers to children's questions about the excluded or the oppressed or the suffering; "always some people have had more and some people have had less" is an example of how adults justify as a natural phenomenon what is a result of a complex history in the human universe.

There are probably many points in common between children and philosophy, but we would like to underline resistance to this natural version of the human universe. Children don't consider many things as natural, in the sense of being determined, normal, unquestionable; they frequently ask why things are the way they are and they tend to see the world in a number of different alternative ways. Philosophy, understood as a radical questioning to the world, shares this same perspective. It is opposed to the idea that any idea, belief, category, practice, value of our social world should be accepted as inevitable or unavoidable. For philosophy, human life is not a domain of natural life. It is an ambit of the not certain, of the contingent, of something that can always be another way than it is. Philosophical questioning puts into question the predominant contingencies, in its foundations, in its presuppositions and implications in order to make it possible to think more complexly about them and about other alternative contingencies to the existing ones.

That's why, among other reasons, philosophy is in so symphonic to children when practiced openly and cooperatively. Because they nurture each other in their search to explore why we live the life we live and what other lives we could build. They help each other asking and investigating the "why" of our contingencies.

Therefore, in their socialization process, philosophy can help children in the constitution of a more self-determined subjectivity. Philosophy can help children to deepen and develop those initial feelings, wonder, curiosity, dissatisfaction that could engender a more complex relation to the world. Philosophy can provide children with the tools they need to be less subjugated to that form of power that tends to constitute them in passive and nonresistant subjects, simply accepting the stories and metaphors that support the actual predominant state of affairs. Then, philosophy can help children to constitute a more free subjectivity that can think more complexly about the ideas, believes, and values that underline our practices and institutions. Understood in this way, the practice of philosophy is an excellent opportunity for children to think about what they are and what they could be.

There is another way to show this same idea. Nowadays, philosophy can help children to face a series of challenges and social pressures for which they are not prepared at schools. For example, they are involved in a series of practices that presupposes a universe of values—as competition, success, dominance—but they are not helped to reflect upon the consequences and implications of these values neither to consider the presuppositions of a world that deifies them. Moreover, our societies are usually contradictory in front of some values. Children are taught to tell and love truth and, at the same time, they are faced with a reality where true has little practiced in front of money or power. Besides, they are not helped to understand what truth means, how many different ways of understanding truth exist, and why it is so important. We don't need to say the truth is just one example. The same could be said of a number of equally significant concepts and values, passed with no coherence and no reflection. Children need to reflect upon the significance of coherence between words and actions and of an entire universe of intellectual categories and practices that configure their perception of the world.

At the same time, through an adequate ambience of collective inquiry, based on cooperative and solidarious relationships children can develop affective and intellectual dispositions that could also be helpful to travel this methodical and problematizing road along with their being at the world.

This relation to philosophy is especially significant for children at the margin of the dominant social system; they need the intellectual and affective supplies in order to think more complexly and thoroughly about their lives. That's why *Philosophy in School* is concentrated on public schools at the social and geographical margin of the Federal District of Brazil, as an imperative of the social, political, and pedagogic commitment of philosophical practice.

5.3 Dimensions and practices in a collective philosophical investigation

We stimulate each child and each teacher to take part in a collective inquiry based on philosophy. That inquiry has at least five dimensions.

5.3.1 Ethical and political

This philosophical inquiry is not interested in the transmission of values and principles, but in questioning and problematizing actual values. This process of questioning implies a number of steps in order to identify underlined values, understand them, question them, reflect upon their consequences and implications, and consider alternative values. We are looking forward to offer children and teachers the tools, resources, and ambience to go ahead with that inquiry.

At the same time, this inquiry is based on several values that are being practiced each time we do philosophy in a classroom:

- *critical questioning*, as way of opening and problematizing ideas, practices, and values;

- *imagination,* as a way of approaching our individual and social reality;
- *participative inquiry,* as a form of building knowledge through an open and founded debate;
- *democracy,* as a form of life that rejects any form of authoritarianism;
- *difference,* as a form of respecting and estimating the other;
- *solidarity* and *cooperation,* as a form of educating, and being educated with, others;
- *radical resistance,* to any imposition, as a form of self-determination.

Certainly, these values are not themselves unquestionable and closed. They are in the process of construction and just a first step from where we propose acting and thinking our philosophical practice with children. In philosophical inquiry there is no space for imposition and authoritarianism and a cooperative and interactive investigation is also expected to question its own basic values. Different points of view are valued, whenever supported by a careful consideration of their foundations. At the same time, these values are not unfounded. Critical questioning, imagination, participative inquiry, democracy, difference, solidarity, cooperation, and radical resistance, as already defined, seem to play a primary role in a philosophical practice committed to thinking and transforming social ideas, values, and practices.

5.3.2   Social

A human being is a social being, constituted through his or her personal and non-personal relationships. In this sense, our philosophical practice tries to foster relationships where children have an active voice and a no less active ear. This means that they are stimulated to express openly their points of view and to consider carefully other's points of view in their own thinking process. They are also stimulated to put themselves in other's places, to take care of the thinking process of other members of the group and to be sensitive to the group voice, without losing importance of their own voice. The group works as a reference so that each one sees its contribution in perspective to that broader respect. At the same time, it is sought that the group stimulates and values the difference of each of its components in an open debate and exchange of ideas affirmed through discourse and action.

5.3.3   Pedagogic

The teacher aids the students in their problematizing search. He or she is not a transmitter of knowledge but a co-inquirer in the path of exploring the philosophical dimension of our being in the world. In that inquiry it is important to examine each position in each assumption, implication, and consequence, whether presented by a child or a teacher.

The pedagogic relationship in this collective inquiry process moves the axis of the attention from the teacher to the group. The teacher is mainly responsible in motivating the reflexive debate among the students and in generating, and taking care of, the appropriate conditions for that philosophical debate to actually occur. It is not expected that the teacher should answer the questions of the children, but she is expected to help them to develop a cooperative philosophical inquiry on those themes.

5.3.4 Philosophical dispositions

We understand dispositions as having three components: tendency, sensitivity, and ability,[1] involving the inclination of a given person toward behavior X, his or her alertness to X occasions, and his or her actual ability to follow through with it.[2] As a proposal for discussion we would like to suggest the following ten main philosophical dispositions to be fostered with children:

1 To put into question actual ideas, practices, and values, not accepting anything as obvious, normal, or natural, but seeing reality as problematic.
2 To identify, understand, and evaluate assumptions, not only looking for what is already there but to what underlies, supports, and is necessarily assumed in what is there.
3 To be sensitive to context, not accepting absolute and careless statements.
4 To openly create and explore alternative points of view, proposing and confronting different and new interpretations and metaphors.
5 To anticipate and assess consequences, looking to human actions as a continuum of related affairs.
6 To think through logical (in its broader meaning of reasoning) rules and principles, being logical rules and principles philosophical, therefore problematic and controversial.
7 To define, apply, and evaluate reasons, examining different ends and world views.
8 To establish ever-more complex (broader) relationships of meaning and sense, looking for an explosion of meaning through cooperative inquiry.

9 To seek for clarity and clear understanding, detecting and appraising ambivalence, ambiguity, confusions, fallacies, sophisms.
10 To resist with courage and perseverance the imposition of any idea, practice, or value.

5.4 A field research[3]

With philosophical practice as a starting point, we propose to investigate the educational possibilities of philosophy, and to help children to question their ideas about what it is to be a child and the relationship between adulthood and childhood, as well as these conceptions' assumptions and implications. We also ask ourselves to what extent philosophy contributes to a more reflective attitude toward what we believe we are and the possibility of thinking of ourselves in different ways.

This field research took place in two public schools in the Federal District: CAIC Professor Anísio Teixeira, in Ceilandia, and Centro Educacional 2, in Sobradinho. The concept of childhood and other topics related to children, their world, their wishes, and so on were investigated through third graders (approximately nine year olds, although in these groups, as in most Brazilian Public Schools, children of different ages are in the same class) through debates held in ten philosophy meetings. The classes were conducted by the researchers along with the teacher of each group. Different texts, such as video, films, children's literature, photographs, slides and others, were used to elicit reflection about childhood.

One of the ten classes is described below:

Date: November 12, 1999
Place: CAIC Professor Anísio Teixeira
Number of students: 35
Theme: Play
Objective: Examine the act of playing
Length of the class: 1 hour and 30 minutes

Facilitator: Angelica

The objective of this class was to make problematic the act of playing. Playing is commonly seen as something obvious and natural. But what do children think about the act of playing? Why do children play? Is it "natural" to play? What are the social functions of dominant "games?" What would children think about this topic? Do children see the act of playing as adults do? What do children say about what adults say about the act of playing?

We tried to give children and ourselves the opportunity to think and question the act of playing, which is something that is often devalued or seen as a "children's thing;" something with no importance which can be postponed, as a popular saying indicates: "duty comes first, then leisure;" or as important only to foster given values such as competition, individual success, and so on.

Class development: the students played freely with play dough, in pairs or groups, as they chose. After playing for 30/40 minutes, the teacher asked the students to comment on their playing. The discussion started from their comments:

> JOSE: "If you didn't want us to discuss you wouldn't have given us time to play, we would've been wasting our time."

Jose's speech suggests that playing is only allowed in the classroom if it has a pedagogical objective. He is saying that in our society playing with no pedagogical aims implies a waste of time; it has no acknowledged social function. We see the act of playing according to its functionality; if there is a function or objective, then it is acceptable. Jose's comment makes us rethink our role as educators and as developers of philosophical discussions among children. Other children came into the scene:

> ANA: "Everything has to be done at its own time. You can't do everything at the same time. The mother determines when it is time to play, and so does the law."
>
> CLARA: "I can determine some things, but not everything. You have to be older to determine things, to tell yourself what to do."

Ana and Clara introduce the discussion about the right time to do things, the time being determined by parents, the law, and older people. Children can determine some things, but being older is a necessary condition in order to have the "right" to decide on some topics. We can notice that a given assumption about children and adult rights is affirmed in both speeches: adults have power, which includes making their own decisions about what to do, whereas children can do only what the adults decide they should do. The child can make some decisions, but only some. These ideas were apparent among all of these groups of children. We developed some strategies in several meetings to enable the children to question these ideas. It was extremely difficult to do so:

> LEO: "I prefer that there is a time for each thing. I think this is good. There must a time for brushing your teeth. I feel lazy when I have to brush my teeth. If there isn't a time for brushing my teeth, I won't feel like brushing them."
>
> JOAO: "If it is time to go to school and I don't go, my mother tells me off."

Leo's statement indicates his belief that if there were not determined times for doing things, he would not do many things that he dislikes or that make him feel lazy; he seems to understand though, that many of these things are necessary, such as brushing teeth. Therefore, Leo does a lot of things he does not like and, in Leo's opinion, having a time for each activity (even though the ones you do not like to do) is good. Since he has to do it, it is better that he has a determined time for doing it, because then he will do it mechanically. It seems that Leo is not given the opportunity to question or participate in the elaboration of the social rules that govern his life. They are transmitted as obligations, duties. Joao confirms that children have no role in making the important decisions concerning their lives. He cannot choose to go to school or not. He has to do it. If not, he knows how his mother would react.

> SARA: "The child is not independent, free like the adult. This is why the adult has to say when it is time to do this or that."

Sara makes a strong distinction between children and adults; the former is dependent, not free; the latter is free. She seems to understand independence as freedom. She is supporting the previous statements made by Leo and Joao: it is because of this that the adult should say what has to be done by children, and when it has to be done:

> SARA: "Playing is doing nothing."
>
> JOAO: "I disagree. Of course it is doing something. If I am playing, I am doing something: I am playing."

In the social scale of values, playing appears as doing nothing; it has no productivity, no concrete benefit. We can relate Sara's speech to Jose's in the beginning of the discussion: "You have only given us time to play because you wanted us to discuss it later." Playing is not recognized as something important in itself by adults. (Even those of us who say we do so and bring philosophy to schools to help children develop a more thoughtful relationship with their own reality!) Joao disagrees with this state of affairs;

according to him, playing is doing something. If the child is playing, she or he is involved in an activity; she or he is not just doing nothing:

> SERGIO: "Children have little time to play, they have to go to school, etc."
> CELIO: "Doing other things doesn't mean that you're spending play time because there is a right time for playing. There's no point in wishing to play in the classroom, you can't."
> JOAO: "I disagree. Doing other things is spending time that you could be playing. I'd rather be playing at home than studying at school."

If adults determine what children should do and at what time, playing can be postponed: it will happen after studying, after doing what adults consider the more important activities. Sergio says that a child has little time to play because there are other activities that must be done first, such as going to school. Playing is not a social priority for adults. Is there a right time for playing? For Celio there is. And it seems to be of secondary importance. Joao again disagrees. He considers playing an extremely important activity and believes that using time that could be used for playing to do other things is the opposite of what children should do:

> CLARA: "Toys motivate children to play."
> ANGELICA: "Why do toys motivate children but they do not motivate adults?"
> CLARA: "Willingness motivates us to play."
> ANA: "There are child things and adult things."

Clara introduces toys to the discussion. According to her, toys motivate children to play. Asked to give reasons for her statement, she introduces the notion of will. It is as if we had a "natural" will to play. Ana seems to mean that when our natural will is influenced by adult culture, it gradually abandons play:

> ALEX: "There are people who discriminate against boys who play with girls' things."
> ANGELICA: "Why?"
> CLARA: "I don't know. When I was born this was already determined: boys' toys and girls' toys."
> ANGELICA: "And how do you know which toy is for boys and which is for girls?"
> CLARA: "We see the toys and know who they are for."
> BIA: "My father doesn't let my brother play with me, with my girls' things."
> ALEX: "My uncle doesn't let my cousin play with a doll."
> SARA: "If you get a doll, will you become a girl?"

The gender issue appears in the discussion. The students did not know how to explain from where this distinction came; when they were born, it was already there. We play with gendered, culturalized toys. For Clara, this is natural, obvious; it is just a matter of "noticing": knowing what toy is appropriate for a girl or a boy is a matter of observing. These ordinary beliefs are produced by means of different strategies. For example, every time a doll or a kitchen appears on television, there's a girl playing with it. There are also girls' or boys' photos on toy boxes. Not to mention the influence of families, as Bia and Alex point out. Sara questions this reality in a very deep way. What is the influence of toys on the player? How do toys interfere with the subjectivity of those who play with them? Jose answers:

> JOSE: "No, but the adults determine what we can play with."
> ANGELICA: "Is it true that the adults determine what you should play with?"
> JOAO: "The child can play with whatever s/he likes, s/he knows what s/he likes."
> PEDRO: "All I know is that we can't tell ourselves what to do, we can't do what we want."

According to Jose, even though toys are not a significant influence on children's subjectivity, adults determine what children should play with. Again, Joao expresses his disagreement: it is the child who knows with what s/he wants to play. Therefore, s/he should decide with what toys to play. Pedro expresses the voice of the oppressed child: even if a boy wanted to play with a doll, that desire would be repressed and he would be prevented from doing so. A child does not have the power to decide what to do.

We'll stop at this point. Throughout these meetings, children had the opportunity to make their voices heard and to listen to one another. Some of them changed their views during the discussions. They analyzed and reflected about their own conceptions about childhood and adulthood. Some children gradually became more conscious of their ability to make decisions concerning their own lives. Some students saw the conception of childhood as problematic and questioned whether adults really know everything (what is right or wrong, what is best for children, etc.).

It was hard for us. Sometimes we were disappointed not to hear what we expected to hear from children about childhood. We were gratified when we heard what we wanted to hear and sad when we did not. We felt the tension between respecting the children's voices and hearing ideas expressed by what seemed to us to be alienated children. If we interfered, weren't we too much directive? If we did not, wouldn't we be collaborators in an oppressive reality?

These questions are still alive; as are many of the questions these children had the opportunity to ask—in some cases for the first time—as part of the gift of philosophy. Might this be a sufficient goal for the practice of philosophy, at this time when so many answers are imposed on children? A place where questions can be constructed and expressed by children themselves.

5.5 Final considerations

In this brief text, an account of the main characteristics, strategies, methods and aims, together with a field experience of *Philosophy in School*, collective project fostered at the University of Brasilia, was presented. The first lines to understand and justify this proposal to introduce philosophy in elementary public schools of the Federal District of Brazil were also drawn. Certainly, we are conscious that many of the ideas introduced here are philosophical and need a more thorough basis and discussion. In the spirit of our project, we don't have the pretension to place ready and finished ideas but to suggest a direction toward a collective construction, developed through philosophical inquiry. As such, it is open, problematic, questioning, contestable, and subject to controversy.

That's the way we build our own way through philosophy and education. Maybe it is because significant problems are not shown and seen as problems at the present time that philosophy seems to be expected to play such an important role among us in the education of children. In this respect, what most specifically distinguishes *Philosophy in School* as a philosophical *project* is this invitation, acknowledged by children, teachers, psychologists, educators and philosophers to participate in the collective construction of a practice where problematizing is much more important than solving problems and affirming a meaningful difference is as significant as resisting the one-dimensional world intended to be imposed. For that, we trust in philosophy and education.

Notes

1 See Perkins, D. N., Jay, E. & Tishman, S., Beyond Abilities. "A Dispositional Theory of Thinking." *Merril-Palmer Quarterly*, Detroit, vol. 39, n. 1, 1993, 1–21.
2 Ibid., 4.
3 This part was developed with Rosana Aparecida Rosana Fernandes. We thank Juliana Merçon for assistance in translating it and Jana Mohr-Lone for revising it.

6
(Some) Reasons for Doing Philosophy with Children

Abstract: *This chapter offers some reasons for doing philosophy with children, derived mainly from the testimony of children practicing philosophy in the project described in the previous chapter. This chapter focuses on a reconstruction of the idea of childhood and its educational condition, starting from the voices of children themselves.*

Keywords: childhood; friendship; otherness; perspectivism; philosophy with children; questioning

Kohan, Walter Omar. *Philosophy and Childhood: Critical Perspectives and Affirmative Practices.* New York: Palgrave Macmillan, 2014. DOI: 10.1057/9781137469175.0011.

I would like to share some of the words spoken by a child participating in the *Philosophy in School* in the Federal District of Brazil, the project mentioned in the previous chapter. Bianca, who is ten years old, was sitting with her friends in a session of what they call "philosophy." They had read the first chapter of Antoine Saint-Exupéry's *The Little Prince*, and they began a discussion of the meaning of drawing. Here is a short transcript from that discussion:

> **THIAGO OLIVEIRA:** The one who explains what a drawing means is someone who looks at the drawing.
> **WESLEY:** That's only sometimes. In mathematics the one who says what is there is not the one who reads, but the signs themselves, and in art the drawing is the drawing, but the one who reads it gives her interpretation, and it is not always the same as the one who made the drawing wanted to say.
> **BIANCA:** Each thing has a reason to be understood why it is understood the way it is understood.
> **DANILO:** If I see a duck here [pointing at a drawing that looks like a rabbit-duck], why would another person say that I am wrong? I am seeing a duck. The drawing is of the observer![1]

Most of the children in this classroom were between nine and ten years old, but some were a bit older. There were almost forty in the class, and about fifteen were participating actively in the discussion. At this point in the dialogue, the problem seemed to be focused on where the meaning of a sign is located—in the author of the drawing, in the reader, or in the drawing itself. Thiago and Danilo seemed to agree that it is the observer who gives meaning to a sign. Wesley agreed in the case of art, but added that there are differences between mathematics and art: in the former, the meaning is in the sign, whereas in art it is the observer who gives meaning to the sign; he also said that an observer might give another meaning than what the artist meant to. Given this context, I would like to explore what Bianca said: "each thing has a reason to be understood why it is understood the way it is understood."

6.1   Two places for childhood

Bianca's formulation seems to me to have tremendous philosophical force. Let's look first at some details: first, "each thing," that is *everything* has an interpretation and, at the same time, every interpretation has a "reason," which is to say something that needs to be understood; there is nothing arbitrary, nothing that doesn't demand an effort to understand why it is understood the way it is. This amounts to something like an omnipresence of reasons (of "why's") for understanding the way in which we understand all things. One might add that some reasons are more explicit while others are more implicit; or that some are more evident, and others less so; or even that some are more or less questionable than others. One might see in this task of making explicit (or non-evident or questionable or thinkable) the implicit (or evident or unquestionable or unthinkable) the proper task of philosophy, of education or, better, of a philosophical education.

But I'd rather proceed a little more slowly. Reading Bianca's sentence again and with a little more attention, it seems to me that she also suggests something like a horizon of meaning and a framework for the search for meaning that shelters and contains the way in which we understand all things. Perhaps even more interesting, she seems to be suggesting that the way in which we understand things is only one way, one form, which leads us to think that there must be many others: there are different reasons and different understandings, and there is a diversity of interpretations and a plurality of reasons for each of them.

The force of this affirmation is enormous and, by now, one might have recognized it as an expression of the main principle of Western aesthetics; another might associate it with Leibniz's principle of sufficient reason; yet another might argue that it is a *leitmotif* of the philosophy of art, and is related to Aristotle's *Poetics*; while someone more interested in contemporary philosophy might suggest that, condensed in Bianca's sentence, we can find the perspectivism of Nietzsche, or the principle of Foucault's genealogy; and finally, one more interested in the origins of philosophy might suggest that something similar can already be found in Heraclitus' second fragment. Interpretations comparing Bianca's statement with philosophical doctrines can continue *ad infinitum*. As a whole, they would emphasize the intense philosophical value of her *dictum*, and we might wonder at how so many philosophers need so much time and so many pages to say something close to what Bianca expresses in such a diaphanous, condensed, and simple way. Fragments such as Bianca's typically greatly encourage those people who argue that children are "naturally great philosophers."

But all these interpretations are contestable. (All have their reasons, Bianca would say!) The judgment concerning the value of children's sayings might be positive, as in our example, or even negative, as is more usually the case in the institutions of philosophy. In a sense, it doesn't make such a big difference. In all cases, the relation established to what a child is saying is the same: it is the object of an adult's interpretation and a comparison with an adult's world. I would prefer not to operate this way in this chapter. I am not offering the "best" or "true" way to interpret Bianca. Rather, I want to think *with* Bianca, trying to hear what she is saying—listening to childhood rather than interpreting it.

Bianca's saying summons us to think the reasons for bringing philosophy to school at an earlier age than our pedagogical and cultural traditions are used to. What in fact are our reasons for doing philosophy with children? Bianca helps us remember that there are diverse ways to understand philosophy, childhood, education, and the relationship between them all, and, therefore, multiple reasons for the enterprise of doing philosophy with children. Bianca helps us to think that perhaps it is important to preserve, to feed, and to take care of this diversity. The reader might not share our reasons, and this is not necessarily a problem. Quite the opposite—if this chapter helps the reader to clarify different reasons for doing philosophy with children, it will have reached its goal. Finally, this is our main reason for writing: in order to think together.

It might be worthwhile to begin making explicit some "other" reasons—relevant and even dominant ones in fact—than mine for doing philosophy with children. At the risk of falling into simplification, I would like to explore some of them, counting as I do on the reader's complicity.[2] Perhaps the most dominant is the notion that philosophy should be in the school in order to help in the political formation of the young. There are different formulas for this idea—for example, "to develop the skills children need to be responsible citizens," "to form the future participants of a mature democracy," "to foster the critical, creative and caring thinking children need to be active members of a democratic society," and so on. We know the words, and in fact the specific words don't matter. The reader might even be able to think in words more acceptable to him or her, in the terms which are the most politically correct for any given context. Whatever the words, what commands our attention is that the place given to childhood, philosophy, and education remains very clear: we make of philosophy a tool for the political education of the young. In other words, we have a model, an ideal *pólis*, and we think that the philosophical education of childhood will help us to realize that *pólis*. Through philosophy, we will form more respectful, tolerant, cooperative children and, therefore, citizens. This is a "formation" model: children are to be formed in such a way as to produce social change; philosophy is introduced into schools in order that, with the help of this modern institution, society might obtain what it does not seem to be able to obtain by itself.

All of these mottos can certainly be genuine and important, but they might not be enough; in any case, they might contain some dangers or weaknesses. First, from a "childish" perspective, the place given to childhood in these formulations does not seem as central as it might be. The grown-ups, the ones who "already know," the subjects of experience, set up the horizons and expect children to reflect them. Of course theirs are the best of intentions, and philosophy is a noble tool for unfolding them. But it is no less true that, in this scheme, childhood's place serves an adult political agenda. Childhood is understood as the human condition which, with the help of a philosophical education, will bring about the kind of world that adults have not been able to bring themselves. Of course, there are lots of versions of this way of constructing childhood within philosophy of education. Some are more coherently democratic, and others even more so; in some others, the theory remains too distant from the practice. In any case, the place given to childhood seems a bit uncomfortable, both philosophically and politically.

The formation model is so strong that it appears almost impossible to think education from another logic. If we do not educate childhood for a given formation, what would we educate them for at all? Besides, models of "education for democracy" certainly look "progressive" in relation to other traditional forms, which are clearly more conservative. Perhaps they are. But we might consider other options. It might not be so impossible after all to think the relations between philosophy, education, and childhood from another logic. Perhaps other reasons could be found, even more powerful in terms of their promise of political transformation. In fact it is philosophy above all that is based in the assumption that things could *always* be different than they are. Are we able to think another place for childhood and another relationship to childhood? We might try thinking from the beginning *with* childhood and children, instead of *for* them. But this statement calls for explanation, and the issue is extraordinarily complex. A whole structure of global understandings of what it means to educate, what philosophy is, and how to think the political dimension of an educational philosophy is involved. Given the little space I have, I'd rather focus on this last issue.

Certainly, we educate from political principles and for political purposes, whether explicitly or implicitly. We affirm values such as freedom, solidarity, or cooperation in our practice. We prepare a space where, for example, it is understood as important to take care of the other, to listen to others' voices; where we subtly encourage and are encouraged to pay attention to what for us is the normal or "natural," and not to problematize it overmuch; to resist all sorts of impositions; to value difference, to foster creativity; and to feel comfortable with a lack of certainties. And the list might continue. In fact we are neither neutral nor apolitical.

But even though we share implicit and explicit political principles and paths, they represent the beginning, not the end. All the principles mentioned above assume that the end is open and are held in such a way that they can enable the participation of the other in a politics that cannot be known or anticipated. In other words, we do not know how the world ought to be, and our "liberal," "progressive" politics is predicated on the notion that all those others who, like children, are excluded should be included in thinking together about how the world might be or ought to be. This in fact is fundamental to our politics.

If we follow, in other words, the logic of our own principles, we discover that the formation principle is in fact a problematic one, and that, once abandoned, we are in a position to operate according to two quite different philosophical and educational principles: first, that education should find its focus, not in the formation of the other, but in transforming ourselves and our relationships; and, second, that our politics is fulfilled, not in the end, but in the beginning and in the process—in the transformation of thinking that enables us to think philosophically together and to think *through* philosophy. On this account, our main reason for doing philosophy with children is to reconstruct our institutions, which implies reconstructing our own sensibilities, as places where children can think as openly, strongly, and freely as possible about what kind of world they want to live in.

In abandoning the formation principle, we put into question the instituted *pólis* and we construct another, philosophizing *polis*, marked by open signs and an unknown future. We do not know what world will emerge from the encounter between philosophy, education, and childhood—nor do we want to. To glimpse it requires time, patience, and careful listening to the voices of childhood. It is true that the Western notion of a "new education" is already very old, but another form of education than the one conceived as formation overcomes even "progressivism." What is called for is another kind of relation between education, philosophy, and childhood, and another politics of education: in short, a childhood of education as well as an education of childhood.

6.2 Another childish example, outside school

Perhaps another example might help us to think about this new structure of relationship. I want to offer an example from my own life with my own children—in this case one of my three daughters—which may be of interest because it happened in a non-educational context. The incident took place during a family holiday in my native Buenos Aires. Milena was nearly three years old at the time. She was born and raised in Rio, so her mother tongue is Portuguese, while mine is Spanish. In Argentina our "normal" condition was reversed: now she was the foreigner, and I had the luxury of talking in my mother tongue. This put Milena in a very "childish situation"—for, being "infant" in the most literal way (*infans*, "not speaking") with Portuguese, whose vocabulary she was just beginning to become friends with; she had almost no word-friends in Spanish.

One day during our vacation, as we spoke together of various things, Milena said: "'tia' in Portuguese is said 'tía' in Spanish." In fact the Portuguese word "tia" and the Spanish "tía" both mean "aunt." The only difference between the two words is phonetic—in the pronunciation of the "t" and the written accent over the "i" in Spanish. In any case, what Milena seemed to be telling me was that she had learned to translate a word from one language into an other. She had discovered that, in what for her was the "other" language, the language of the other—Spanish—there was an equivalent for a word she already knew in her own language; and further, that words could mean the same, although they were pronounced in different ways in the two languages.

I smiled with joy. Milena had shown, not only that she was intensely involved in learning her own language, but that she was also able to speak more than one language! I must have uttered at least two or three expressions of admiration, and with barely a transition my pedagogical pretensions overtook me—and, as it turned out, played me for a fool. In fact the idea came to me immediately that this moment represented a magnificent possibility to "deepen" her learning. After all, so many years of teaching could have not passed in vain, nor did I want to miss an "opportunity" for Milena to exercise her analogical thinking. So, in a manner rendered somewhat anxious by my eagerness to provoke learning, I asked her: "Milena, if 'tia' (in Portuguese) means 'tía' in Spanish, then, how do you say 'tio' in Spanish?" Surely, I thought, a simple analogical transition from feminine to masculine would deepen her structure of understanding!

I have to confess that I was already prepared for an experience of intense pedagogical joy; in fact I could hardly contain myself. The professor in me rubbed his imaginary hands, like those hunters who sense that their prey already has one foot in the snare. I had, I thought, only to wait. Milena appeared to me so clever, so magnificent (the way we usually perceive our own children), and I thought she would answer the question easily. It was only a matter of "facilitating" her learning. In fact this, finally, is the core notion of the "progressive" pedagogical speech all around us these days—that children should construct, with our help, their own learning, that each moment of learning should give rise to another significant moment of learning, that true learning is "learning to learn," and so on.

Sadly, my confirmation did not come. I continued watching Milena expectantly, and there was no answer! I must have repeated the question a couple of times, barely suppressing my anxiety and impatience. Milena was delaying the "next step" (my step, as it turned out). Finally, after seconds seemed to have stretched into hours, Milena, watching me, smiling, said with a calm and diaphanous smile: "Tio in Portuguese means 'amigo' in Spanish." Of course "tio" means "uncle" and "amigo" means "friend." Milena had not answered what she ought to have answered! Mercifully, I was able to take a deep breath, to contain myself in the face of this new otherness, and said nothing—simply smiled nervously. By rare psychological luck, I thought to myself that I had better chew a bit on what Milena had given me before considering any next step. When I was calmer I could think more about this lesson from a foreigner of two years.

Milena had not responded the way I wanted her to. Milena did not give the expected answer—one of the things children learn to do in school. But Milena is a living, thinking being. She said what she thought, in a direct, clear, and unpretentious way. Her answer resisted my instructional logic and my predictive pretensions, the same logic and the same pretensions that inform the dominant pedagogy. Fortunately for both of us, Milena *thought*, and her thinking made me think. It surprised me with a sudden, joyful energy. She had helped me to see what I did not seem to be able to see for myself.

Before sharing what I learned with Milena, one clarification is necessary. As in the case of Bianca, I am not going to fall into the temptation of interpreting Milena. In the case of Bianca, I gave a few examples of how her words could be imported into the sanctuary of the history of philosophy, and no doubt other disciplines might be tempted to find their particular truth in what was said in both cases. For example, a sociologist might say of Milena's intervention: "Surely she made that analogy because in Brazil 'aunt' has a very different cultural and social connotation than in Argentina." A psychologist might consider the following interpretation more perspicacious: "Milena said that because she has a more close affective relationship with her uncles than with her aunts." And a semiologist might try to deliver the "true" understanding of Milena's words: "By the word 'friend' she meant the following: ...." In fact the interpretations of why Milena translated "tio" as "friend" and not as "uncle" might continue indefinitely. Everywhere there would appear fortune tellers of her "real intentions, meanings or cultural devices." Nor would their interpretations lack meaning, and they would provide us with tranquility enough. Yet—and perhaps exactly *because* of the slightly uncomfortable satiety of the "tranquility" offered by all these social devices for interpreting childhood, or just because we might consider that children deserve the opportunity to think differently—I would prefer not to take any of these paths. After all, it would be silly not to accept the opportunity that a child is giving us to think; to lose that opportunity would be of no educative value whatsoever.

Thus, rather than attempting to explain what this particular child-foreigner meant, I will try to think *with* her statement, to open myself to what she can teach me; instead of constructing the child as an object of my knowledge, I will construct her as the subject of a knowledge I do not have. I will understand her to be at my own level, an equal with whom I can enter into a dialogue. I will take this sentence of hers as a point of departure from which to re-think my relationship with the foreigner and the child and—why not?—with a certain foreignness that inhabits myself. What follows is what, from this perspective, I thought from what Milena said, in five brief sections.

6.2.1 Thinking's beginning: friendship

There is no thinking without friendship. The well-known etymology of "philo-sophy" (and all the compound words that begin with the Greek form *philos*) might be a help here. Milena suggested an inversion of the usual way of reading this etymology: it is not a question of being a friend (*philos*) of knowledge, but of knowing what friendship is. Friendship is not only a path for knowledge to walk along, but also something that needs to be cared for in order to know, and in order to participate in a form of thinking that deserves the name. Friendship is both a condition and a beginning for thinking: both an old and a new beginning; we do not think except in a friendly environment. I am not speaking about personal relations, as we commonly understand the word "friend," but as a condition of possibility for the act of thinking for oneself and with another.

Milena helped me to think that the conditions of thinking do not belong to the institution of the family, but to the institution of friendship—and she did so precisely in the context of a familial relationship. The definition of a friend in Aristotle's *Nichomachean Ethics* (IX, 1170 a) might help to reinforce this idea: *philos allos autos*, which can be read in three ways; a friend as: (1) another same one; (2) another same self; (3) an other-same. In this principle of friendship, a world of alterity and sameness is opened in the realm of thinking. Certainly questions proliferate: what or which kind of friendship? Friendship for what? Friendship between who and who? Or between what and what? These questions suggest the force of Melina's principle: a disruptive, creative beginning of a new world in thinking.

6.2.2   Paying attention to the asking

How do we relate to the other? How do we stand before the child-foreigner? We occupy the terrain of knowledge and of power—the knowledge of power and the power of knowledge. We ask questions that do not really question, that do not question ourselves. We ask about what we already know, and what we don't know we don't ask about. We question without questioning, because we already know, or we think we know. We listen only to the answer that confirms our knowledge, that leaves us fixed in the same quietly comfortable land of certainty. We ask in order to listen only to the answer that confirms us, the answer we know before asking the question. We ask the other, the foreigner and the child, what we would never ask ourselves: the question which, because we know its answer, we do not think it necessary to rethink. We ask questions to the other to listen to ourselves, and we only listen to ourselves in the other.

We ask questions to the child-foreigner like a school evaluator: in order to verify that the other knows and thinks like us, to be sure that he or she learns the knowledge we already know and, in last instance, to show her everything we are capable of if she does not know what she ought to know. We ask as if we were test-givers, dedicated only to checking the already fixed answers, without truly asking. We question the other without questioning, as we watch without watching, think without thinking, and live without living.

6.2.3 A new sense of the foreign

To learn is to translate. To translate is to invent. To invent is to invent ourselves. To invent ourselves is to listen to what we do not listen to, to think what we do not think, to live what we do not live. Childhood speaks a language that we do not listen to. Childhood pronounces a word that we do not understand and that we do not care to understand. Childhood thinks a thinking that we do not think and that we do not care to think. To give space to that language, to learn that word, to really care about that thinking can be an opportunity, not only to establish a fundamental place for the word of childhood, but to take *us* to a new, foreign land. Listening to childhood's voice offers the opportunity to stop putting others on the outside and going *ourselves* to the other land, to the land of the other, to leave our comfortable place for a while, and—who knows?—to transform what we are. That, it seems to me, is the force of childhood: to present us with a new language, a new land, a new self to think and to be.

6.2.4 The affirmative force of childhood and of the foreign

Milena was in a foreign situation for a child. It might be seen as a restrictive one: she could not speak "her" language. But in fact it turned out to be a field of possibilities for her. To be abroad allowed her to learn new words, new thoughts. It showed that the foreign can be a force, a power as much as a limit. The foreign is something that has the power to mobilize and cause changes, in ourselves and in the others around us. A proper and convenient situation for learning—the foreign can be that.

Milena also showed me that childhood—*in-fans*—can be something very different from what the etymology of the word suggests: the *in-fant* pronounced her word, resolutely, without requesting permission, without asking for authorization. She thought and said what she thought. And that childish word and thinking gave me the force to think. A power, a force, a capacity that thinks and helps us to think—this also is childhood.

6.2.5 Philosophy for Children

What does this short example tell us about this practice called "Philosophy for Children"? I think that it might help us to think both about the principles and about the various forms of doing philosophy with children, just as Bianca's did. In effect, both examples help us to think beyond or behind the practice, to think in a way that has not so much directly to do with the "how" as with the "why" and the "what for" of philosophical practice with children. It seems to me that doing philosophy with children can help us to put into question ourselves through those foreigner-children. It is something like an exercise in the foreign—a practice that allows us to hear what we do not hear. In that sense, it allows us to become another kind of teacher than the one we are, and above all helps us to arrange other kinds of spaces and places for the foreign childhood that we need to educate. In other words, that childlike scenario can give place to a living exercise in the affirmation of the foreign, and in so doing can help us, not only to think differently about the education of childhood, but to provide a space for a childhood of education—a new beginning, a new earth, a new thinking in the realm of teaching and learning.

6.3 The word of a less literal childhood

I would like to finish with another testimony, this time from one of the teachers who took part in the same project, *Philosophy in School* in Brasilia. This particular teacher had almost no academic formation in philosophy, since in Brazil, like almost everywhere on this earth, philosophy plays a marginal role in the educational formation of the young. In this case, one of the teachers who accompanied the children in their philosophical practice, Délia, a childlike teacher of childhood, spoke in one of our teacher workshops about her relationship with philosophy and the meaning that philosophy had come to have for her daily practice. Délia affirmed that philosophy allows us "to think and to rethink our practice...it is the beginning of our philosophical way, a way that never ends."

Once again, I will not emphasize the profound philosophical content of this sentence, nor will I try to show how close what Delia said is to such and such thinker, or to what I think philosophy is. Instead, I would prefer to think *with* her and *from* her.

Délia emphasizes the proximity between philosophy—thinking—and the practice that she thinks: we mainly think our practice, and we think it again and again; we think it and we return to think it once more; we repeat the gesture of thinking our practice, and in that gesture we think and we return to think ourselves. The gesture of thinking is repeated in a way which does not repeat itself—it unfolds a complex repetition, a repetition of the different rather than the same. In other words, we think in order to be able always to think in another way, to renew the pathway of thinking, and the reasons we have reserved for ourselves in order to understand ourselves and the world in the way we do, as Bianca would say. Such a way, Délia suggests, is a way that a teacher begins but never ends, since it accompanies a whole life. A philosophizing life is a never-ending search.

Where Délia locates philosophy on this route is interesting, as well as the image she uses to talk about it: philosophy has the form of an unending path. Philosophy is located, not at the beginning as the origin or foundation, nor at the end as totalization or universality, as it is usually pleased to represent itself. It is not located at the place of arrival, at an end, a completed purpose, because there are no such points of arrival. Neither foundation nor purpose: philosophy is always on the way of beginning the path of thinking, and on the way of continuing this route; a way of taking us from one place to another; a rite of passage—that is philosophy for this teacher. It is what allows us to leave the place where we are and to reach another place; to leave off occupation of an old land and to reach for a new; it is an interruption of location in thinking, and something that makes bridges, that finds its way between two distant points. Philosophy is thus a form of childhood in the realm of thinking.

The path of philosophy is thus an unfinished and endless path in thinking. Practiced with children, it offers the possibility of finding and perceiving oneself in the middle of what one is looking for. It helps maintain the route, to not forget one's beginnings, to value the absence of certainties, to notice the many ways, always present and unfulfilled, which are still there to walk, to explore some of them. All attempts to complete philosophy fail: there is no way to foreclose the enigma of thinking, the mystery of what we are and what we could be. In doing philosophy we accompany that enigma, maintain it, feed it, but we cannot mitigate it. It is neither necessary nor advisable to be frightened by that enigma, for it would be like being frightened by ourselves. To provide for childhood (whether, in a literal sense, as the first stage of life, or even in another sense, as a possibility of experience) the path of philosophy presupposes that we are disposed to coexist with that enigma and that absence of certainties; it also presupposes something more—that we are ready to allow children to make their own way while taking the path.

As always, an endless number of questions remain open to think, and there is one in particular that I find difficult to forget: Is it possible that philosophy as I have represented it can occur at all in the realm of school? Is not school—that classical institution of modern power and discipline, as Foucault taught us (1997)—the space *par excellence* of the control of thinking, of naked political hierarchy, of lack of freedom and absence of transformation?[3] Isn't there a mutual incompatibility between school as an institution imposed and administered by the dominant order, and any attempt to philosophize in a rebellious and childlike form within it? Isn't school the negation of open, free, and revolutionary thinking?

Perhaps it is, perhaps it isn't. We don't know, really. I find an enormous number of children and teachers who—at least in many places in Latin America—work diligently, under the severest conditions, to maintain the possibilities that philosophy as I have construed it embodies. It is meaningless to anticipate answers. Philosophy and childhood are matters of experience, and for this reason it is preferable to leave the question open. Everything makes its own experience. As Bianca said, "each thing has a reason to be understood the way in which it is understood." Each idea, and each person too. Out of these experiences new reasons can come to life. We will welcome them. All the thinking in this chapter arose from listening to Bianca, to Milena, to Délia. To childhood. To the other. To those we usually think of as having nothing to say to us. Can we imagine what might happen if we gave more attention to those whom we think have nothing to say to us?

Notes

1 The transcripts—together with some others—can be found, in Portuguese, at www.unb.br/fe/tef/filoesco and also in Juliana Merçon's a paper entitled "History and sense of a project." *Childhood & Philosophy*, vol. 1, n. 1, Jan./Jul. 2005.
2 What we here call traditional way to think the relations between philosophy, education, and childhood has been focused in Part I of this book.
3 Foucault's studies on discipline in the modern institutions can be seen in its already classic *Surveiller et punir* (1997). On the productivity of Foucault's studies to education, among the so many works can be consulted with profit, for example, S. Ball (ed., 1990).

7
Philosophizing with Children at a Philosophy Camp

Abstract: *This chapter narrates the experience of educational philosophy the author undertook with Korean children at a Philosophy Camp in Seoul. After describing this experience, the chapter considers the meaning of doing philosophy with children everywhere, and questions some purposes commonly affirmed for this practice, in educational discourse: (a) education for citizenship; (b) forming people capable of an (intelligent) adaptation to the labor market; (c) something enjoyable in itself, which does not require other justification.*

Keywords: Heraclitus; philosophical inquiry; philosophical practice; philosophy with children; Zapatism

Kohan, Walter Omar. *Philosophy and Childhood: Critical Perspectives and Affirmative Practices.* New York: Palgrave Macmillan, 2014. DOI: 10.1057/9781137469175.0012.

A dozen invited guests from different countries had an opportunity to participate in the Philosophy Camp, July 31—August 3, 2008, at Seoul National University as part of the XXV World Congress of Philosophy. It was organized by a team led by Professors Duck-Joo Kwak and Ji-Aeh Lee. For the event, the Philosophy Campus was sectioned into different groups, each one meeting four days for two hours each day, with invited professor from abroad and a group of no more than twenty volunteered Korean children from all over the country. The groups were divided by age, starting with eight-nine year olds. I had a rather small but intense group of around ten children in the first two days, and around fifteen children in the following, who were eleven–thirteen years old. I also had two assistants, with whom I communicated in English—Lee Ji Young and Choi Jae Wan, both highly committed and sensitive to our work. They also helped with translation, even though most of the Korean kids could express themselves in English, or at least could understand it.

Coming from such a different context (I am a native of Argentina, and have lived in Brazil since 1997), it was difficult for me to plan and prepare my activities with Korean children. First, I did not know them, either personally or culturally, so I could hardly imagine their context or their expectations, both of which are so important to planning any pedagogical activity. Second, I was eager to place myself in a position from which I could respond to their expectations in terms of "learning philosophy" or having a "philosophy class," and at the same time enter into a dialogue with them—that is to say, be sensitive to their own thinking and, if possible, not only teach them but also learn from them. In fact, it is at the balancing point of these two attitudes where, I have found, doing philosophy with children is most interesting: in a space where we think with others instead of convincing them or trying to make them to think as we think, where we undergo the possibility of thinking differently ourselves through entering into dialogue with them. This is also the educational power of philosophical practice—an experience in which at least two voices join to think together, and through this encounter, to think what they had not thought before. If this fact is especially important when an adult encounters children, it is even more significant in this particular case, where the "Western" adult encounters the "Oriental" child (or the Oriental child encounters the Western adult). It would be quite a good opportunity, I thought, to put myself and my own culture into question, and to help them to put their own into question.

With this aim in mind, I prepared some introductory activities the first day, in which each person in the group would introduce himself or herself to the others by giving himself or herself a nickname and explaining why that particular nickname. At the same time, each group member would choose one animal into which he or she would like to reincarnate, or would like to have been in a prior life, or with which one simply identifies oneself with. All of these activities would, I hoped, provide us with a more relaxed and intimate atmosphere: it would help the students feel less tense in terms of the forms expected in a "philosophy class;" it would let us know some intimate aspects of each other; and at the same time it would make us to begin thinking about the topics that would be presented for discussion during the course, as will get clear in the following.

After the introduction, which was lively and animated, I asked the children to engage in an activity. Children would go around the classroom to "search" for something. I did not tell them what they needed to find, if anything, or if they had to search in any given specific way. I was purposefully vague in the formulation of this command because I wanted the topics proposed to be a product of the first part of their own search. Some bookmarks—written in a strange alphabet, and thus not easily "understood" by the students—were "hidden" in obvious places, and if someone displayed them as a result of their search, my colleagues and I would ask them if they had ended their search, or if there was still space for the search to be continued. Throughout the activity, as often as we were asked clarifying questions, we asked them to clarify their own clarifying questions, in order to help them to think about the meaning and sense of their search. After some minutes, we brought the students back together, and asked about for what and how they searched, and about what, if anything, they had found. We also explored the relationship between searching and finding and some questions were raised, such as "Does finding always follow searching?" "Can we find something without searching it?" "Is it always the case that we find something because we search?"

This activity was directly linked to the text that was introduced next, "The Story of the Search," written by the Mexican Sub Marcos, one of the leaders of the EZLN (the Zapatista Army for National Liberation). This text (which I include as Appendix A at the end of this book) was read by all the participants, who had formed a circle, and read one paragraph each. Briefly put, the story narrates the creation of the world from the accounts of different traditions—mainly from the ancient cultures that inhabited America previously to the violent invasions by Europeans in the fifteenth century. The story also narrates the creation of different species, and conveys a sense of the world as something incomplete, full of "undone things." Every human being is born unfinished, and the task of every person is to find himself or herself. We are born lost, and as we grow up we seek ourselves. The story also provides a basic guideline as to how to go about looking for oneself: by walking the other's road. Sharing this story was important to me for many reasons: it was a way of (a) giving my students a taste of the rich tradition of Latin American culture; (b) enlarging their understanding of philosophy to encompass more than the usual canon of texts (the Greeks, Descartes, Kant, Hegel, etc.); (c) offering them a different world view, coming from an interesting contemporary movement (Zapatistas). The story is a rather open one, non-dogmatic and full of philosophical elements.

After we read "The Story of the Search," I asked the children to discuss the story in small groups, in order to think about the points that caught their attention, and to formulate questions concerning any of the issues related to the story. The list of questions that they made was as follows: (a) Why is each person finding themselves as an unfinished thing? (Ironman & Nintendo); (b) What can we do to find ourselves? (Rabbit & Disney); (c) According to "The Story of the Search," we find ourselves as we grow up. What happens if we die without having found ourselves? (Doraemong & Smile); (d) Most of gods depicted in a religion or fables are absolute and complete. But why did the gods in this story leave things that were uncompleted? (Sabang Devil); (d) What is the meaning of finding oneself? (Sky).

It is interesting to note that all of the questions indicate a deep understanding of the story and a strong capacity for problematizing what they have read. Some of them built on what the story affirms, but others put the assumptions of the story into question. We discussed these questions for some time, and as we finished, I asked them to think of a word that might, in some way, express something about what they had searched for and/or found during this class. They were particularly interested in thinking about the meaning of the words we were using (search, find, completeness, incompleteness, goodness) and pursued this inquiry with passion and strength. What was particularly interesting for me was the fact that we were doing something very close to what we were discussing: the connection between searching, finding, thinking and living was present, not only in the text, but in our conversation; in fact we seemed to be searching within ourselves through thinking with each other. And the children seemed to enjoy it so much! We were enjoying the very path of philosophy—moving from questions to other questions through answers that were continually put into other questions.

On the second day, we read a selection of fragments from Heraclitus. We did this in a circle, each one reading one fragment at a time. We read around fifty fragments (I realized it was probably too much, but I did not want to give up the opportunity to offer them such strong thinking). I asked the students to choose their favorite ten fragments out of those fifty, then I asked them to pick five out of these ten, then three out of these five, and finally one out of these three. I asked each student to read the fragment that he or she had chosen, and justify the choice. Fragments centering on issues of life and death counted among most favorites. The reasons for their choice were also interesting: for example, (a) people are afraid of death (Smile, for fr. 27); (b) because it has do with death (Disney, for the same fr. 27); (c) It described the cycle of life (Doraemong: for fr. 88); (d) It is interesting to think that everything changes (Nintendo, for fr. 6); (e) Thinking about what to do is interesting (Rabbit, for fr. 16); (f) It says that the human beings are the most beautiful (Shabang Devil, for fr. 82).[1]

After that, I asked each child to render the fragment they had chosen through a drawing, and to write down a question. What follows is a summary of some of the presentations of the drawings and of the questions that emerged from them:

NINTENDO: I tried to describe the sun that never stops changing in our eyes.
Q: How do we know that the sun changes every second?
IRONMAN: I drew a cycle of life and death. They complete each other.
Q: What do you think not dying is? Living forever or just living before death?
RABBIT: I described a thing that never sets.
Q: How can we hide from something that never sets?
DISNEY: I drew a dead person crossing the river of death in a boat.
Q: Is there anything scarier than death for humans?
SHABANG DEVIL: I described how humans are more beautiful than the monkeys.
Q: What is the criterion of beauty?
SKY: I drew the sun that becomes new everyday
Q: Why does everything change?
DORAEMONG: The fragment that I picked is somewhat like recycling.
Q: Do life and death circulate forever?

SMILE: People do not imagine death.
Q: Why not?

We ended this second session by reading all their questions, and I invited them to think about them for the following day. All the activities of this day were individual, and we only rarely entered into group interaction.

When some of the children asked me if they could read something for the third day, I suggested that they read Plato's *Apology of Socrates*. At the beginning of this meeting, I asked them if they had been able to read anything and, to my surprise, some of them had! After listening to what they had enjoyed about it, I offered them a short summary of Socrates' judgment and death, and I put some questions to them, thinking to connect the story with the questions they had made about Heraclitus, and to push our thinking process a little further. I questioned them about the meaning and the forms of life and death, and about the relationship between these concepts and how they themselves related to them. I also told them what Socrates says about life and death in the *Apology*, and I asked them whether they agreed with him when he suggests that we don't need to fear death because we don't know what death is, and that it could be like a quiet sleep or a continuation of life. After this introduction, a long and sustained conversation followed for about an hour and a half. The following dialogue was part of this conversation (Vélez was my own nickname):

DISNEY: I am afraid of death because people might forget about me.
VÉLEZ: Why be afraid of something that you can't imagine?
NINTENDO: We are afraid of death because we observe others' deaths. People want to last long, but death is an end.
BAT: People are afraid of death because they don't know about it.
VÉLEZ: Why be afraid of things we don't know? Couldn't it turn out to be better than when we are alive?
BOOKDOOCHILSUNG: Everybody believes that his world is perfect but when he dies, you can never come back.
RABBIT: I fear death because I will have to stop all the things that I used to like to do [...] people want to accomplish something, but when you die, you will not be able to.
IRONMAN: I believe that life and death circulate. Life is like playing during the day and death is like sleeping. No one likes to go to sleep early.
SKY: Not everyone's life is a happy one. People do kill themselves, and if they were afraid of death, they wouldn't kill themselves. Some people are afraid of life.

NINTENDO: I am not afraid of death. People will die anyway, and not every death comes in the same way.
IRONMAN: I think we are afraid of death because it comes unnoticed.
VÉLEZ: Are we afraid of things that we cannot control?
ALIEN: Being afraid of death is like being afraid of the dark. But just like we don't need to be afraid of the dark, we don't need to be afraid of death. Maybe we are not afraid of death itself but of the process of death.
NINTENDO: It is true, but death is scary because people who were close to me would be sad when I die. However, we all die anyway so we need not be afraid.
VÉLEZ: So we need to distinguish between the reasons why we are afraid of death. First we need to differentiate between death itself and the process of death, second between the worry about oneself dying and the worry of how sad others will be if one dies. Are you still afraid of death?
DORAEMONG: It is scary to live in this world forever.
NINTENDO: Let's say we could live forever. We would feel like a rich man who will never lose his money.
[...]
IRONMAN: Eventually, scientists will invent pills that will make people live forever.
VÉLEZ: If there was such pill, would you take it?
IRONMAN: I would because I want to live forever. I want to meet those I have been with all along. We don't even know what will happen next we die.
VÉLEZ: Then, wouldn't it be sad to see others die and disappear? Wouldn't you think that it's unfair for some people to die and some people to live forever?
BOOKDOOCHILSUNG: We feel pain during life. I don't want to feel pain forever.
ALIEN: Because the pill will be very expensive, there will be people who can't afford the pill even if they want to buy it.
[...]
CHICKEN: death is fate. So it is immoral for humans to have control over it.
VÉLEZ: Would we still be human beings if we didn't die? Isn't living eternally to become god? Also, people can invent pills that stop us from dying, but they cannot invent pills that stop us getting in a bad accident ...
DISNEY: Judging who would die and who would not is up to gods. It is immoral for humans to decide it...
IRONMAN: Why do we need to follow what gods decided for us?
ALIEN: I don't think this issue has anything to do with gods. They will not bless nor punish us if we take the pills or not.
VÉLEZ: Then when do we need to take the pill? Can we invent pills that make a bad person into a good one? If we didn't feel anything, would we still be human beings?

BOOKDOOCHILSUNG: Taking the pill would mean going against the law of nature.
ALIEN: It would be boring to live the same lifestyle if we took the pill that makes us immortal.
[...]
CHERRYPINE: If we are always happy, then it wouldn't be a feeling that human feels.
IRONMAN: Why do we have to live forever as humans?

The conversation was exciting and energetic, but at this point I realized we had only some minutes to finish it. So I asked them to work in small groups, each group identifying one thing that all the members of the group agreed they had learned during this discussion, and formulating one question that could push our conversation further. This is what they said they learned, and what they questioned:

GROUP A (ALIEN, SKY, SHABANG DEVIL): People not only fear death, but also the process of death.
Q: What really is death?
GROUP B (NINTENDO, CHICKEN): We learned that we do not know death but we fear it.
Q: Why do we fear death?
GROUP C (CHERRYPINE, SMILE): If we live forever, there is no meaning to living life as human beings.
Q: Would people want to live forever in spite of losing meaning as human beings? Are people born with certain value as human beings?
GROUP D (RABBIT, PETERPAN): People are afraid of death because they tend to believe the things they can see, but death cannot be seen. We have no knowledge of what happens next.
Q: Would people be happier if the pill that makes us immortal were invented?
GROUP E (DORAEMONG, BOOKDOOCHILSUNG): We learned about two views that Socrates had about death.
Q: Would people's lives be determined by their wealth if the pill was invented?
GROUP F (BAT, IRONMAN): There are always up-sides and down-sides to things that are seemingly good or bad.
Q: What if all people became extinct before scientists could invent pills that made us live forever? If many people start taking the pills that make them immortal, things such as natural resources will eventually run out, then won't we be living in a technology-only world, like robots?

For the last day, I decided to bring the concept of the body more into the scene of philosophy, and to stress the concept of life. We worked with "The three metamorphoses," that short section at the beginning of Nietzsche's *Zarathustra*[2] which proposes three forms of archetypical life—obedience, criticism, and creativity. Introducing this reading was also a chance to offer the students a piece by a strong, more contemporary philosopher. We read the text a few times, and then we did some exercises in which we expressed with our bodies the metamorphosis of the spirit narrated in the text, from camel to lion, and finally from lion to child. This section of *Zarathustra* is particularly interesting because the child is declared to be at the end and not, as is more usual, at the beginning of a process of formation (or transformation); because of the concept of transformation that guides the passage from the beginning to the end; and because it enables us to embody the thinking process, and to reflect on the relationship we usually have with our own bodies. We did the latter through individual exercises of imaginative body transformation, through silence, and through reading short texts produced by the students, as well as revisiting fragments from Heraclitus. This was followed by a group presentation of four skits created by as many groups, each developing its own understanding of Nietzsche's transformations. The two hours passed very quickly, and this session ended the course, immediately after which we participated in the closing ceremony of the Philosophy Camp, where one of the groups presented the skit it had just created.

7.1 The sense of doing philosophy for and with children

I have described this experience in such detail because I think it can help us to think about the meaning and sense of doing philosophy for and with children. The issues surrounding the latter project are certainly complex, and I do not want to discuss them thoroughly here, but simply offer some notes on the practice that bear further development or reconsideration. I would like to start by citing three meanings that are usually attached to doing Philosophy for Children. Of course they are not the only possible ones, but they are—at least in my context—the most influential in educational circles. In effect, when justifying why one should do philosophy with children or why one should introduce philosophy in schools, three main answers are offered: (1) as a contribution to an education for citizenship (or democracy, or any other political concept); (2) as a way of formatting people who are more capable of an intelligent adaptation to the labor market; (3) as something enjoyable in itself, which one is not obliged to rationalize or justify.

I find each of these arguments problematic. As regards (1), the relationships between philosophy and the city (or polis), philosophy and politics, and philosophy and democracy are problematic. Even from the birth of philosophy,[3] as Socrates testifies, the politics of philosophy are opposite to the politics of politics. The contribution of philosophy is a contribution to thinking, and this contribution has always been seen as politically useless or even dangerous, as Socrates' life clearly indicates, and as Plato claims in a number of dialogues, such as *Gorgias* and *The Republic*. So it does seem to be doing more for philosophy than it ever claimed to do to present it as a contribution to democracy or any other purely civic value. For philosophy, democracy, citizenship, and politics are things to be questioned, not end points of its practice.

If the first proposition makes philosophy dependent on politics (democracy), the second makes it dependent on economy (capitalism, the market). Here the effect on, and the risks to, philosophy are the same, particularly in our time in which, due to the intense development of capitalism, it seems that the market can and does prevail over everything else. In the market, everything can be bought and sold, and everything is expected to have a price. "Philosophy for Children" is not at all immune to being transformed into a commodity that is offered and sought after, submitted to the logic of consumerism, used as a marketing strategy, sold as a product that can differentiate one educational institution from another, and so on. But again, for philosophy *any* given economic system is something to be questioned and not something to which it needs to adapt. For philosophy, capitalism and market are issues to be questioned, not to be automatically accepted as "the way it is."

If the first two propositions put philosophy in the unpleasant position of having to acquiesce to a different regime of thinking, the third one puts it in the unpleasant place of someone who feels so superior to the others that he or she does not need to give account of himself or herself to anyone. And even though this position has been defended many times in the history of philosophy, it is has no attraction for anyone who sees philosophy as a social practice, and its actors (mostly professors of philosophy) as people with duties and responsibilities like any other.

As a philosophical and educational project, "Philosophy with Children" needs to be considered philosophically, with as few non-thinkable points as possible. In fact the justifications for doing philosophy with children are very closely related to the way we consider each of the terms in the name of the enterprise—"philosophy" and "childhood"—and their conjunction. Of course, the issue is so huge that I cannot do more in this chapter than offer a few ideas that could be pursued further. Above all, we might do well to avoid idealizations or universals, such as the ones present in phrases such as "Children are natural philosophers," or "Philosophers, like children, question everything." Such slogans tend to suggest an abstract vision of philosophy and childhood: that the universal "child" and universal "philosophy" are naturally related. It would also be well, I think, to avoid the fundamentalism, dogmatism, or moralism implicit in understanding philosophy as an instrument for passing down a set of unquestionable values. The latter can be done, after all, either in the name of reactionary or progressive values, using the most beautiful and vile words, the most seductive and the most scandalous.

What is childhood (infancy, *infantia*)? Judging from its etymology, infancy has usually been considered as a lack, absence, or deficiency, and the education of childhood as a dispositive that would fill that negative space. Due to childhood's lack of structure, education has therefore been thought of as the formation of the unformed, the filling of the empty, the development of the undeveloped. Maybe it is time to look at what childhood *is*, its presence and forces: what emerges from birth, the force of looking at the world as if it were the first time, the experience of the unaccustomed, the eagerness for meaning.

If infancy as absence has given space to education as formation of childhood, and if the result has been an educational system based on discipline and control, it could be that infancy as presence opens room to a childhood of education, a new beginning for the enterprise, where attention and sensitivity recover their fair place. And, as a practical exercise of transformative thinking *with* children, philosophy can play a transitional role in this historical passage from the education of childhood to a childhood of education.

The example of the Philosophy Camp at Korea—because the others involved were such different others to each other—offers an interesting opportunity to think about the relationship between childhood and philosophy. Its value for reflection is not by way of a lesson or a model, but rather as an opportunity for a shared learning experience. Childhood is not only—or not predominantly—a stage of life, but a force of experience. It is the strength to turn into a new form of experience. It is not something that we should be concerned to form through an educational experience, but what makes an experience of (trans) formation possible. Beyond any list of intellectual abilities, habits, or dispositions we might attribute to it, childhood requires our attention, openness, and sensitivity.

Notes

I thank my friend and colleague David Kennedy who polished the English of this text.

1. Numbers correspond to Diels-Kranz edition.
2. This activity was inspired by my colleague and friend Ricardo Sassone, professor at the University of Buenos Aires.
3. Even though before Socrates there was a lot of philosophy, with Socrates was born a forma of philosophy linked to dialogue and question with, and to, others.

8
Does Philosophy Fit in Caxias? A Latin American Project

Abstract: *This chapter describes a project of practicing philosophy with children in Duque de Caxias, Rio de Janeiro, Brazil, which is taking place at present (2014). These pages explore this project's creative and unique ways of educating children (and adults) through philosophical experiences of thinking.*

Keywords: creativity; ignorance; philosophical experience; philosophy with children; Public Schooling; teacher education

Kohan, Walter Omar. *Philosophy and Childhood: Critical Perspectives and Affirmative Practices.* New York: Palgrave Macmillan, 2014. DOI: 10.1057/9781137469175.0013.

This chapter introduces an educational and philosophical project that is still very much alive and in process. The project "Does Philosophy Fit in Caxias? Public School Bets on Thinking" —is housed in two public schools in the city of Duque de Caxias, a suburb of Rio de Janeiro, Brazil that may be characterized as an urban poverty zone. The project involves philosophizing with students *and* the creation of a teacher education agenda in which teachers study and practice the art of facilitating philosophical experiences with their students. Created in 2007, it is sponsored by the Center for Philosophical Studies of Childhood (NEFI) at the University of the State of Rio de Janeiro (UERJ) and includes roughly twenty teachers and 400 students from ages six to seventy—with the latter as part of an adult literacy class.

The teacher education plan includes several workshops ranging between twenty and forty hours each. The workshops occur within the schools and in residence on the campus of UERJ on the island of Ilha Grande. These workshops are mainly experimental and sessions have basically two forms: "experiences of thinking" and "thinking the experience." The former are initially conducted by the coordination team and progressively by all participants with their support throughout the planning of the session. They consist in philosophizing as a process of "problematizing," "dialoguing," and "conceptualizing." Each session is free to choose its strategies, texts, and so on as soon as they unfold the mentioned triad. Along with the workshops, the program includes regular meetings at the designated schools and at the university. Students of pedagogy and philosophy at UERJ also take part in these activities. The participating students attend workshops at the university, and they and their teachers have participated in two international conferences organized in Rio. Since the beginning of the project, one teacher has completed a Master's thesis that takes the project as an object of research, and two others are in the process of doing so.

Though still relatively new, this project has received significant attention. TV Escola—a national educational network—has produced a one-hour program on the project, and a book on it has recently been published (Kohan & Olarieta, 2012). There is also an Internet site dedicated to the project and its work (www.filoeduc.org/caxias). The project demonstrates that extra-campus extension activities are as essential to the university's mandate as are teaching and research. Rather than the transmission of knowledge from university to community, extension is here understood as a form of research in which "insiders" and "outsiders" together think through the problems and opportunities with which the experience of philosophy presents them.

8.1 Paths to experience philosophizing

Given the centrality of collaborative philosophizing in our project, our goal has been to organize an experience without pre-determined methods or curriculum materials, and to approach pedagogical practice like an artist, who needs not only skill and practiced sensibility, but also a radical openness to the world. Materials and techniques are at service of the pedagogical setting just as they are for a musician or a painter. We offer principles, texts, and philosophical questions to teachers as materials that each one works with in his or her own way. None of them is inflexible, nothing has always to be included or avoided—they represent elements for thinking about the "what" and the "how" of philosophical practice. We list some of our shared action principles or "gestures" in appendix B at the end of the chapter.[1] What follow are some theoretical principles that sustain our project.

8.2 The importance of the awareness ignorance

The understanding of philosophy that we affirm was born with Socrates to the extent that his practice was a public exercise of the word, through questioning and problematizing. Dissatisfied with the dominant ways of life in the *pólis*, Socrates called them into question, and pushed his fellow citizens to confront their problematic assumptions.

Importantly, Socrates was understood to be wise because of his relationship with ignorance;[2] he was aware of his ignorance, and this made him the wisest person in Athens. Even knowing that he would never reach a consolidated form of knowledge, he doggedly sought it. He lived to search and searched to live a life worth living. Importantly, Socrates never claimed to be a master of anyone. He did not transmit any knowledge, but he generates learning. In this way he suggests a stance for the philosophy teacher: one who causes learning without claiming the status of a teacher; not being a master, his followers emerge.[3] The Socratic position is inspiring in the way it opens a space for the practice of educational philosophy as a living exercise of thinking, instead of as a transmission of knowledge. This means that the teacher does not plan philosophical experiences aiming to transmit knowledge (or "values" or "competences" or whatever) to his or her students but because of the meaning and sense of thinking experiences themselves and the learning they eventually might generate.

Another inspiring figure for our philosophy teacher education perspective is Simón Rodríguez, a Venezuelan of the nineteenth century, named by his disciple, Simón Bolívar, "The Socrates of Caracas."[4] Like Socrates, he was a relentless critic of his society, calling its foundations into question, walking around the city confronting the dominant ways of life. He also dedicated his life to "educating" people—interrogating them, challenging them to seek out other possible worlds. Like Socrates, he criticized the masters as transmitters of knowledge who equated education with a technique for the dissemination of knowledge. He also was a disturber of the social status quo, with a pedagogical, philosophical, and political project of transformation. Both the Athenian and the Caraqueño spoke a language other than their contemporaries, both were considered exotic, extravagant, strangers in their own city, and ultimately dangerous to the established order.

The Caraqueño said "We invent or we err."[5] The claim is philosophical, pedagogical, political, and existential. To truly educate all the people, in knowing and doing, for a common life to come which is as yet unknown, we cannot rely on any dominant models of education. We must invent it. Any imitation will reproduce the logic of submission and extermination that has reigned in Latin America for centuries. Monarchical schools teach sophisticated skills of reasoning, such as the Aristotelian syllogism, to justify the subjugation of the Indians. Instead, we must educate the real owners of the land, those dispossessed by the colonial power. We must think feelingly, painting a reality of freedom for all the inhabitants of our own terrain. The truth is not out there waiting to be discovered; rather it is part of an ethics and a politics that can make this part of the world a place of true freedom for all who inhabit it, a place like no other on earth.[6] Following Rodríguez, our program seeks to rethink the notion of education from the ground up, to work with individual and groups who have been marginalized or subjugated, and through shared philosophizing to envision a future reality for all of us. Particularly with adults-students we emphasize the philosophical disposition of making our experience of the world strange, of seeing the ordinary as extraordinary, of finding no naturality or normality in culture, concerns that would be unlikely to be raised in the given process of schooling.

8.3 Intellectual equality between teacher and student

Everyone has an equal capacity to learn (Rancière, 1987/1991), everyone is able to do what any human being is able to do, affirmed J. Jacotot a couple of centuries ago.[7] The same intelligence operates in creating a piece of art as in cleaning the street. This principle—simple, difficult but also clear—disrupts the normalization process characteristic of the school. The teacher is not supposed to explain what he or she knows and have students to accept it: each one must seek and find for themselves, in the company of others, their own way. This is what a true teacher cannot fail to know or practice—that he or she needs to learn and teach so as to generate learning that the other wants to provide himself or herself. It is necessary that the other learn, first, that he or she is able to learn and think like everyone else. The teacher needs to know that in terms of capability, his or her intelligence is no more and no less than any other intelligence, whatever difference in experience and any other respects they have. As such the teacher's entire task reconfigures itself. It is no longer supported by the knowledge that has to be transmitted, or the skills that the other must achieve, but in caring for the way the other wants to learn. What matters is that the other wants to learn, to seek, and never stop seeking. It also doesn't matter *what* the student learns—what matters is that he or she learns and keeps learning forever, with full attention. There is nothing we should expect the student to learn except to continue learning; and there is no method to this other than the student's. So that philosophical experiences aim to provoke the seeking of experience and thinking itself. They do not aim to "teach to think" but the will, desire, or inspiration to "learn to think" and keep learning to think endlessly.

8.4 Emphasis on experience?

Inspiration for our project also came from French thinkers such as Foucault, Deleuze, and Derrida. From Foucault comes a tentative relationship to claims of truth, and a wariness about the modern disciplinary structures of schools and how they affect individuals within them (Foucault, 1997). From his thinking, we suggest that the teacher's task is not only to transmit truths but also to question, by experience, his or her relationship to truth (1994b: 41). The idea of experience inhabits the practice of philosophy considered as an exercise or experience of thinking, in which form and content are always mutually imbricated, continuously trying to think in another way without consecrating or legitimizing what is already thought and known, but always searching to think and learn in other ways. In doing philosophy together, we not only learn about ourselves, but we also hear from others. Foucault, like Deleuze, taught us the indignity of speaking for others.[8]

In this way, we stop thinking of education as a training device to promote certain forms of subjectivity by means of a normative discourse on what ought to be, and begin to think it as a friendly, introductory practice of opening spaces that disrupt the dominant dynamic in schools so that teachers and students can take part in new forms of being and, in Deleuzian terminology, to new becomings. We also learn to differentiate between childhood and children, and to mistrust the form of temporalization that divides life into chronological stages. There is no univocal correspondence between teaching and learning—someone can teach with nobody learning, and someone can learn without anyone teaching. Finally, we learn that the teacher who pretends to be a model teaches nothing: we only learn with those who propose gestures that are sensitive to difference.[9]

Derrida (1990) also teaches us to see the paradoxical relationship between teacher and method. A path is needed, as well as planning, resources, texts, sensitivation strategies, evaluations. But philosophy escapes from any method. The best method used in the most accurate way may not provoke a philosophical experience, which can occur *against* a method, or with an anti-method.

8.5 Taking philosophy outside the university

From Giuseppe Ferraro—a Neapolitano and a friend—we learn the necessity of taking philosophy outside the walls of the university and into the city, and even into the outskirts, at the extremes, where it seems to have always been absent, yet which is its more proper and vital space. We learn that philosophy can only be practiced among friends, because rather than simply being a quest for knowledge (as the word is commonly translated) philosophy is a knowledge of desire, of searching and of friendship. Philosophers do not philosophize together because they are friends, but they become friends when they philosophize together (Ferraro, 2010a: 5).

Ferraro teaches that philosophical knowledge is not about things, but about the taste[10] that these things have, how and why we feel them in one way and not in another—the way they are, what they are and nothing else. Philosophy helps us to think if someone or something is being what he or she or it truly is, if he or she or it lives a life with the strength and joy that could be living. Philosophy is a way of looking at what we are, and thinking whether we are what we truly are. It is a sort of interior gaze, provoked by the encounter with other perspectives, which moves us to understand and transform what we are. It is a form of affection—both to affect and to be affected—of bodies thinking together (Ferraro, 2010b: 18).

Ferraro also teaches us that philosophy can be a way to find, together, in concert, the voice of words. It is at the edges of the city that the excluded voice finds its words in experiences of philosophy. It is only at the outskirts, where it doesn't seem to be able to be what it is, that philosophy finds out what it truly is. For philosophy, to leave the walls of academia is not a promenade; it is the possibility of being truly itself (Ferraro 2010a: 8–9).

8.6 Philosophy for *Children*

Matthew Lipman created the contemporary form of *p4c*, and with it a very large philosophical movement emerged. Ann Margaret Sharp worked tirelessly to disseminate the project. The very idea of our project is inspired by Lipman and Sharp, if only by the original formulation of the possibility and the crucial importance of putting philosophy and children together in educational institutions. Although we do not adopt their program, and even affirm significant differences in our way of conceiving philosophy, childhood, and the sense of how they meet, we have learned much from Lipman and Sharp.

Among other things, we have learned from them to place the utmost importance on the coherence between what we think and what we do, and on the form of our practice in educational institutions. This is a crucial issue in teacher education, which is no longer thought of as the transmission of theoretical and methodological supports, but as a site where we practice ourselves what we expect to practice with students. The practice of philosophy turns on the experience of *questioning*, and immersion in philosophical practice assumes an implicit trust in its transformational power. As such, philosophical practice represents a major challenge to the traditional educational position of the teacher that mainstream institutions insist on spreading (Lipman, 1988: 11ff.). Lipman and Sharp have led us into a process of learning to unlearn how to be a teacher, all the while remaining open to the emergence of new, affirmative ways that are revealed by the experience of philosophy in action.

The idea of community of philosophical inquiry is essential to this process. Philosophy is not an individual's lonely, introspective, reclusive task. It may be so in another space. But in the common meeting, it is quintessential dialogical practice, where what matters is not to have the truth or to quote the masters, but the voicing of the collective inquiry, which tends always to show the complexity of the problems under discussion, and different ways of approaching a question, or of attempting to think it through. Above all, in community of inquiry, philosophizing becomes an opportunity to meet with each other—with other thoughts and with the thoughts of others (Lipman, 2003: 81ff.).

8.7 Philosophy as rebellion: "it's enough!"

Subcommandant Marcos is the intellectual leader of the Zapatista movement, which erupted in the Lacandona Jungle in the Mexican state of Chiapas in 1994. Marcos is a university graduate in philosophy who at some point of his life traveled from Mexico City to Chiapas to live the reality of oppression and exclusion of the indigenous Chiapanecos, and in this experience to build a singular political movement of resistance to that reality. From the Zapatistas we have learned, above all, a way of thinking state politics. The meaning of Zapatista politics is inscribed in the epigraph, "Today we say 'it's enough!'" presented in the First Lacandona Jungle Declaration, on January, 2, 1994 (EZLN, 1996: 33).

"Today we say 'it's enough!'" indicates a period of time—500 years—during which ancient Mexican indigenous people have fought against the invaders, who stole their land, their food, their wealth, their lives. It also indicates an action in the first person plural: *"we say."* A collective voice, one people, a common force that expresses resistance: words as a form of rebellion. Finally, it indicates a loud voice, an exclamation, a cry that breaks the apparent calm, the silence. It is the sign of a limit, a point that cannot be passed beyond; a marking to this ancestral time that justifies and gives a meaning to it. The Zapatistas announce a new policy: no excluded ones, no hierarchies, no false representations. In this policy, there are no longer those who command and those who obey, those who know and those who are ignorant, those who legislate and those who abide by the laws. Zapatism is an equality politics asserted by the fact of difference. Our philosophy project adopts this general stance, and infuses the work of Marcos in our philosophy discussions. Marcos wrote many stories—for example, "The Story of the Search," "The Story of the Looks," "The Story of the Mirrors"—which bring together elements of pre-European American mythologies and contemporary European thinkers, and which are inspiring texts for philosophizing with children.[11] They show a complex, open, incomplete world, in which human life requires thinking for oneself and with others. The Zapatista movement also makes us see policy in more colors, because Zapatistas not only write stories and letters, but embody the life they are becoming through music, painting, costume, street theatre, and media spectacle. The strength and pain of " 'it's enough!" affirms a colorful expression of life.

Philosophy as a creative sensibility: The last of our inspirations is a Brazilian poet — Manoel de Barros — an artist and creator from the epic tropical wetlands of the Pantanal. In fact the sense and feeling of the philosophical experience that moves us comes very close to that of the artistic experience: the tone of creative sensibility. In addition, Barros is an inventor of infancies, of a special relationship with childhood, both in his writing and thinking. His presence is very strong in our practice. He inspires us with the beauty of the writing and the creative exercise of his thought—aesthetics and invention bound in each other's service. The epigraph that heads his volume of poetry—*Infancy: Invented Memories*— serves as a manifesto: "All that I do not invent is false" (Barros 2010: 3). For Barros, as for Simon Rodriguez, invention is a criterion for truth. It may be that not all inventions are true, but if all we do not invent is not true, then we also know that something that we do not invent cannot be true. Creation is the gateway to the world of truth.

The poet of the Pantanal has taught us to unlearn a diminutive and schematic view of childhood, opening doors for a more powerful, rich, and complex one. The child's world in his writing is one of intimacy with things and the world, in a "child block" of vital force and creative energy. His poetry shows the strength of a childlike form of being and seeing the world. He teaches us the ugliness and poverty of the diminishing gaze so often applied to childhood, and finds a special strength in the thinking associated with attending to what normally is regarded as small or useless. Read with equal pleasure by students and teachers, his writing breaks down disciplinary boundaries and methodological strictures. His texts lead us into a rich, powerful, and beautiful exercise of thinking. Let's consider, for example, his poem "A didacts of invention," where he offers a number of examples of how to touch the intimacy of the world. In the last sentence he affirms: "To unlearn eight hours a day teaches the principles" (Barros, 2000), which is in fact the principle of our work. Because of his irreverent relationship with syntax and grammar, which demands that we unlearn a standard form of writing, he also inspires us to think beyond standard forms, and thereby beyond the world in which they constrict us, to other possible worlds.

Notes

1. These examples have been taken and rewritten from NEFI (2011: 58ff.).
2. This presentation of Socrates comes from Plato's, *Apology of Socrates* (20dff.).
3. 'Socrates' presents this argument against the accusation of corrupting the youth in Plato, *Apology of Socrates* (33a–b).
4. See letter from Bolívar to Santander, from Pallasca, December 8, 1823. In Rodríguez (2001c: 117).
5. This phrase appears many times in his writings. Cf., for example, Rodríguez (2001c: 185).
6. This idea is developed in *Sociedades Americanas*. In Rodríguez (2001a: 193ff.).
7. The principles of Jacotot are presented in the first chapter "Une aventure intellectuelle," in Rancière's *The Ignorant Schoolmaster* (1987/1991).
8. This is affirmed by Deleuze in an interview with Foucault, "Les intellectuels et le pouvoir." In Foucault (1994b: 309).
9. Cf. the Introduction of *Différence et Répétition* (Deleuze, 2003/1997).
10. Etymologically, to taste (*sabor*) and to know (*saber*) share the same root in Latin.
11. These stories can be found in http://enlacezapatista.ezln.org.mx/

9
Philosophy as Spiritual and Political Exercise in an Adult Literacy Course

Abstract: *This chapter explores the educational possibilities of an experience of philosophy with illiterate and marginalized students in a public school taking part in the same project described in the previous chapter. It also presents a practice of reconstruction of the childlike subject, who is not a chronological child but a chronological adult experiencing a childlike education through philosophy.*

Keywords: dialogue; literacy; Pierre Hadot; public schooling; spiritual exercises; text

Kohan, Walter Omar. *Philosophy and Childhood: Critical Perspectives and Affirmative Practices.* New York: Palgrave Macmillan, 2014. DOI: 10.1057/9781137469175.0014.

9.1 Introduction

This narrative describes and problematizes one year (2007–2008) of educational and philosophical work with illiterate adults in contexts of urban poverty in the Public School, *Joaquim da Silva Peçanha*, located in the city of Duque de Caxias, a suburb of the State of Rio de Janeiro, Brasil. The project, "Em Caxias a Filosofia En-caixa?!" ("Does Philosophy Fit in Caxias?!"),[1] involved a teacher education program in which public school teachers studied and practiced the art of conducting philosophical experiences with their students, and the authors' experimentation with philosophical experiences in an adult literacy class. This narrative concerns the latter aspect of the project. The thirty students and two teachers involved in the course did not study the history of philosophy, nor did they create philosophical systems or theories. Rather, they participated in a philosophical experience that might best be understood by examining Pierre Hadot's concept of philosophy "as a way of life"—a notion as old as Socrates. In the *Apology*, when defending himself against the accusations leveled against him by his fellow Athenians, Socrates uses the word "philosophy" not as a noun, but rather as an infinitive verb (29c) and as an adverb (23d, 28e, 29d) that qualifies his manner of living, for which he is being persecuted. Philosophy then, appears to be a kind of practice, a form of living in which one "examines oneself and others" (*Apology* 28e).

The "philosophical way of living" practiced by adults in a public school literacy class is discussed and examined in this narrative. The narrative also aims to demonstrate that: (a) a "philosophical way of living" can be practiced by any adult regardless of literacy ability or number of years of formal education; (b) philosophy as a lived experience can be a transformative practice that contributes to what Paulo Freire calls "the reading of the world" and is thus an epistemological and political condition of critical political literacy; (c) there is a reciprocal relationship between dialogue and a "philosophical way of living" such that each cultivates the other; and (d) in spite of conditions, tensions, and challenges, there is indeed space within schools to inspire and nurture a "philosophical way of living." In other words, even if there is no formally recognized place for "philosophy as a way of life" within schools, assuming that this way of life can be practiced within classrooms can generate transformative practices within these institutions.

"Em Caxias a Filosofia En-caixa? A Public School Gambles on Thinking"

The philosophical experiences under investigation in this chapter occurred in Duque de Caxias, a sprawling city of 870,000 inhabitants roughly thirty minutes outside the city Rio de Janeiro. Joaquim da Silva Peçanha Public School serves one of the socio-economically depressed zones of the city. The school consists of around 800 students aged six–seventy years, and functions from 7:00 am until 10:00 pm five days a week. In 2007 the school administration and nine teachers from the school decided to begin work with the Center of Philosophical Studies of Childhood (NEFI) at the State University of Rio de Janeiro (UERJ) on a project that aimed to create and nurture philosophical experiences in the school's classrooms. The project, "Does Philosophy Fit in Caxias?! A Public School Gambles on Thinking," involved six members of NEFI working with individual teachers for one year inside and outside of their classrooms. Several workshops—between twenty and forty hours each— were offered by members of NEFI during the first year of the project. On a weekly basis seven teachers involved in the project philosophized with children (ages six–fifteen) in their classrooms. Two other teachers, Graça and Monica, coordinated a weekly philosophy class with thirty adult students (ages seventeen–seventy) enrolled in a nightly literacy course.

The majority of the students enrolled in the adult literacy class worked full time during the day and studied at night. Many were immigrants from other states in Brazil who had migrated with their families to the state of Rio in search of work. Enrollment in the literacy class did not mean that students had to participate in the weekly, one-hour philosophy class. Attendance was optional, and all students were asked to give their oral consent before the year-long course began. No student had ever taken a philosophy course before. Many, we later discovered, had no idea what the word "philosophy" could mean when they had agreed to participate. Nonetheless, attendance during the course was consistently over 90 percent and the majority of students enthusiastically requested to continue with the course in the 2009–2010 academic year. In fact, as we write this chapter (November 2009) a dozen teachers from three other schools within the same school district have joined the project, with support from their municipal Secretary of Education. A new group of adults has entered the project, and has participated in philosophical activities in their school and at the State University as well.

9.2 Philosophy as spiritual exercise

The question "What is philosophy?" like all philosophical questions is an open and controversial one. Each philosophical enterprise has its own way of answering it. Even though it is endlessly open, an examination of two major works of Pierre Hadot, *What Is Ancient Philosophy?* (2002) and *Philosophy as a Way of Life* (1995), reveals an approach to answering this question that has been very meaningful throughout the history of philosophy, and for our work: philosophy can be conceived of as a number of *spiritual exercises*[2] that transform the way we see and live in the world.

In what follows, the nature of philosophical *spiritual exercises* as presented by Hadot is briefly summarized and examined in the context of the project just described. By re-visiting one year's worth of philosophical experiences with a group of adult learners we can outline and ruminate on the characteristics of *spiritual exercises* and how they contribute to a "philosophical way of living" in adult education courses. More broadly, we can consider how the practice of philosophical *spiritual exercises* can nurture more dialogical relationships with oneself and with others. Finally, we consider how practicing philosophical *spiritual exercises* has significant political consequences.

There is a classic and significant difference between learning the history of philosophy, or being introduced to *philosophies*, as theoretical discourses and philosophers' systems, and actually *practicing* philosophy (Hadot, 2002: 2–6). The former typically demands that students begin studying the classic philosophical works written by the great thinkers of ancient Greece and work their way chronologically to the influential thoughts and texts of today's contemporary philosophers. Along this linear and chronological trajectory students are exposed to different sorts of explanations meant to interpret and give account of theoretical discourses. There is, of course, a strong value in learning this philosophical tradition; and, to some extent, any rigorous engagement with philosophy needs to take into consideration that tradition. If philosophy is an "on-going conversation" in a Rortyan sense, there is no way to enter that conversation without being aware of its history. Nevertheless, frequently teaching and learning the philosophical tradition becomes an end in itself, and too often this path of study cuts short philosophy as an experience or practice.

In contrast to this academic approach, Hadot has demonstrated that philosophy is above all a way of life, one that demands an *askesis*, a Greek word meaning "exercise" or "practice" and is capable of transforming the individual engaged in it. Thought of in this way, philosophy is a *spiritual exercise* that intends to effect a modification and transformation in the subject that practices it (ibid.: 6). It is a practice intended to carry out a radical change in our being. It is an exercise in which thinking takes itself as its own subject matter and seeks to modify itself (ibid.: 82), and thus to provoke a radical change in the individual. Yet, philosophy as a *spiritual exercise* is not situated merely on the cognitive level (ibid.: 83). It is a determinate way of living which engages the whole of existence; it is a conversion which turns our entire life upside down, changing the life of the person who goes through it. In sum, the object of *spiritual exercise* is to bring about the possibility of transformation.

In a course of lectures given between 1981 and 1982 entitled *The Hermeneutics of the Subject*, Michel Foucault (2001: 2–39) built upon the concept of philosophy as *spiritual exercise* to affirm that it is only through what he calls the *moment cartésien* that philosophy in modern times turned out to be understood merely as a cognitive exercise. In spirituality, however, there is no way of building knowledge or reaching truth which does not pass through a transformative practice or *askesis* of the self. Foucault relates this shift of philosophical practices to the concepts of "self-care" and "self-knowledge." While in ancient Greece "self-care" was a broader conception of the relation individuals have to themselves, of which "self-knowledge" was only a part or dimension, gradually throughout the centuries there was a movement that made "self-knowledge" the privileged relation to oneself, and one not necessarily tied to a moral or spiritual project of self-care. Each category affirms a different relationship to truth: while in a culture sensitive to "self-care" there is no way to access truth but through a moral discipline of the self, in the modern "self-knowledge" culture, access to truth is merely a cognitive discipline which does not involve any transformation of the subject.

Within the context of a "self-care" culture, some ancient thinkers provided inspiring lists of *spiritual exercises*. For example, Philo of Alexandria left us with two lists that include the exercises of thorough investigation (*skepsis*), reading (*anagnosis*), listening (*akroasis*), attention (*prosoche*), and meditation (*meletai*).[3] These *spiritual exercises* cultivate a way of seeing and being in the world. They do not entail the transmission of pre-determined knowledge from one person to another, nor do they constitute a methodology which guarantees epistemological certainty and existential security. Rather, the philosophical experience cultivated by *spiritual exercise* is an individual and shared journey of inquiry, discovery, and transformation—one that calls oneself into thought, one's way of being in the world. It is such a journey that thirty adult students and two teachers in the city of Duque de Caxias decided to partake in.

9.3   Spiritual exercises in Duque de Caxias

A short list of the *spiritual exercises* that were practiced in the adult literacy course in Caxias includes the practice of asking questions that call oneself into thought about being and the nature of the world, engaging in dialogue with oneself and others, cultivating a disposition that accepts uncertainty, doubt and mystery, exercises of "being a child"[4] and "taking flight each day," and making oneself eternal by surpassing oneself (see Friedman, 1970: 359, cited in Hadot, 1995: 70).

These exercises were not the result of strict adherence to a prescribed teaching methodology. Nevertheless, some clarification is needed. In a sense, problematizing has been the core of our practice and informed the way we worked. During remarks that this was also the core of Aristotle's philosophical practice: "the most characteristic feature in Aristotle is his incessant discussion of problems. Almost every important assertion is an answer to a question put in a certain way, and is valid only as an answer to this particular question" (1964: 97–8, cited in Hadot, 1995: 105). Aristotle's method was to continuously problematize and approach each problem from different angles; each problem receiving contemplation specific to it. Socrates and other ancient philosophers were also adherents to this practice. "Such a method, consisting not in setting forth a system, but in giving precise responses to precisely limited questions, is the heritage—lasting throughout antiquity—of the dialectical method, that is to say the dialectical *exercise*" (Hadot, 1995: 106). Many contemporary philosophers, such as Bergson, also give importance to problematizing and the way one responds to each problem raised: "It is true that philosophy then will demand a new effort for each new problem. No solution will be geometrically deduced from another. No important truth will be achieved by the prolongation of an already acquired truth" (Bergson 1946: 20). G. Deleuze, who was heavily influenced by Bergson, points out that philosophy consists in a three-dimensional activity: (a) setting forth a plane of immanence; (b) bringing a problem into this plane; (c) creating a concept for that problem (Deleuze & Guattari, 1991: 15–34).

So, even though there was no prescriptive method to our philosophizing practice in Caxias, it was guided by the principle of problematizing.

In addition, all of the *spiritual exercises* in Caxias shared certain elements. Each began with the engagement of a text which had the ability to call the students into thought by provoking questions, which were discussed and ruminated on. Text, questions, and dialogue—three of the key elements present in all of the philosophical exercises in Caxias—were not meant to transmit pre-determined knowledge or guide the interlocutors to arrive at pre-determined epistemological objectives or goals. Rather, they were meant to cultivate an individual and shared thinking experience in which questions were more valued than answers, and doubts and uncertainties were expected to be more transformative than scholastic expertise. A brief inquiry into each of these elements follows.

9.4 The text (texting and self-texting)

Is it possible to work with texts in a class of students who cannot read or write? It is if we reconsider what we mean by "text." A text is anything that calls for interpretation or reflection. It can be a drawing, a picture, a photograph, a conversation, or a life situation that is reflected upon. Texts are signs that need to be interpreted and put into question in order to be more deeply understood. Moreover, the world and our individual and social experience of the world are, as Paulo Freire clearly demonstrated, texts that need to be interpreted. As Freire states: "The reading of the world precedes the reading of the word" (1992: 11). The world is a text and a critical reading of it enlarges our perception. Ontologically and epistemologically speaking, the reading of the world comes first: there is no way to give sense to a word without giving sense to a context that nurtures that word. At the same time, however, the reading of words continues and develops the interpretation of the world (Freire, 1992: 20).

In our course for adult students the stories and experiences that the group problematized were very much a product of the world that they had "read," and that they wanted to discuss and question with others. Following Freire, we might also speculate (we have no empirical evidence to support this) that this "reading" of the world, this problematizing of the world, and philosophically discussing the "world as text" with others, eventually leads to a more profound relationship with literacy, which, in turn, leads to a more profound relationship with the world. The world and words are read in a deeper way. One might say that our perception becomes more insightful *after* having had the chance to philosophize over the "world as text."

This type of "reading" has political implications. Freire (1992: 21) states that the critical reading of reality, as part of a process of learning to read, associated with political mobilization practices, could make up a part of what Gramsci would consider counter-hegemonic actions. Thus, philosophy as an exercise of critically reading reality opposes itself to other forms of education that foster conformity and maintenance of the status quo. It is a practice that empowers the subjects of this practice to have a much-more complex and active relation to reality.

The act of reading the world as text is a singular experience of thinking, impossible to repeat exactly. This is even more so when practiced with illiterate groups. The oral nature of the texts and discussions make each experience with philosophy a new experience because the "text" changes as the participants in the experience change. As their reading of the world changes, their reading of the "words" also changes.

As such, the subjective dimension of the philosophical experience is reinforced. Philosophy re-enters its Socratic path as a living conversation directly addressed to a limited audience in an oral way. In the *Phaedrus*, Socrates points out some advantages of orality in contrast to writing (Plato, *Phaedrus*, 274c ss.). The subject can choose to whom he talks, while the author of a written text loses control over who has contact with the text—it is the reader who chooses the text he or she reads. Another advantage pointed out by Socrates is that oral discourse can be revised and corrected, while written text is fixed and impossible to alter. A third advantage is that oral conversation preserves memory while written text weakens it. All of these dimensions of oral texts could be experienced in our dialogues in Caxias. With these students, philosophy was an ongoing process, a shifting back and forth and hence a process of always re-creating texts, thinking, and ways of living. Unknowingly, our group of students was revitalizing an ancient form of oral philosophizing.[5]

In Caxias the "texts" that instigated our philosophical experiences were often the life experiences of the students themselves. Similar to oral communities that share wisdom and knowledge through story-telling, our dialogues often involved students relating paintings, photos, and songs to their personal life experiences and then problematizing them individually and as a group.[6] Individual life experiences became the "texts" that created communal philosophical experiences.

The word "text" has the root meaning "to weave" and it is, Walter Ong tells us, "more compatible etymologically with oral utterance than is 'literature' which refers to letters (etymologically/*literae*) of the alphabet" (2002: 13). Oral discourse is a form of weaving or stitching—*rhapsoidein, rhapsodizing*—which basically means stitching songs together (ibid.). Adult literacy courses that foster dialogue as a means of learning and sharing wisdom have something in common with the ancient Greek concept of *rhapsodizing*. The human experiences that are stitched together and "sung" in oral communities become texts that are capable of provoking questions that call the community into thought and that put them on the way to philosophizing. Thus, it is possible to say that the creation, interpretation, and discussion of such texts are practices that can be considered *spiritual exercises*. According to the Italian philosopher Giuseppe Ferraro (1990), these exercises do not simply mean procuring a meaning that is present in a text; they also involve the reader finding his or her own voice in the text. Our practice of oral philosophizing in Caxias therefore involved exercises of self-texting: encountering one's voice in the text that the world offers.

9.5 Questions (questioning and self-questioning)

If philosophy means, as Karl Jaspers has claimed, to be "on the way" then we must ask what puts us "on the way" (1959: 12). Or if we associate philosophy with a kind of thinking that puts us "on the way," we might ask "what is it that calls us into thought?" In the ancient Greek tradition, we are put "on the way" by philosophical questions. Our being in the world needs to be questioned if we are to have a thoughtful and meaningful existence. Philosophical questioning concerns itself with this being, with the way we interact with the world, and our experiences in the world. Every experience becomes a potentially boundless experience when it is put into doubt, but is de-limited by the philosophical question. Thus our experiences with the world, with ourselves, and others are completely changed by the act of asking philosophical questions. We begin to see and interact with the world, ourselves, and others differently only after we have questioned them. According to Foucault (2009: 83), Socrates' task of making others question themselves was a way of provoking them to care for themselves. We could also say that questioning the world around us makes us break with our habitual way of inhabiting the world, and opens the possibility for caring for the world. Finally, questioning other people and our relations with them makes us re-think how we relate to them. In short we can say that putting our lived experience and our being under question is a *spiritual exercise* that is a potentially transformative experience.

It is of great importance to note that the journey in questioning/problematizing, according to Hadot, "is not the solution of a particular problem, but the road travelled to reach it" (1995: 92). Hadot argues that this emphasis of journeying with questions is clear in Plato's dialogues. One spends a long time in the company of these questions and expands great effort, in which one "rubs names, definitions, visions and sensations against one another" (ibid., referencing *Letters VII*, 344b; 341c–d). This relationship with questions is exemplified in Plato's so-called Socratic Dialogues and also in some of the later dialogues such as the *Statesman* (285c–d). Socrates affirms that he has nothing to teach, no knowledge or content (*mathema*) to transmit (*Apology* 33a–b). Nevertheless, he is committed to continuous questioning and dialogue with others, the purpose of which is not arrival at a pre-determined answer but the therapeutic practice of dialogue itself.

Ruminating on philosophical questions within the context of our work in Caxias we can expand upon what it means to be "on the way" in philosophy. Very often external observers have asked us: "Are these questions that the students are asking philosophical? What is a philosophical question then?" In response we affirm that if philosophy is a *spiritual exercise*, then it is not the questions themselves that are philosophical or not philosophical. Rather, what we tried to cultivate in Caxias was a philosophical relationship to questions, a certain spirit that would allow questions to question our being in the world, to let ourselves be questioned and eventually transformed by journeying with the questions themselves. We fostered questioning and self-questioning. More than the act of asking philosophical questions, what the *spiritual exercise* of questioning cultivates is a state of "being in question." In this sense, the art of self-questioning (not questioning something external, but putting oneself in question while questioning) is the core of our practice.

By far the greatest challenge of the Caxias project was the difficulty students had in forming questions which would provoke this kind of self-questioning and, at the same time, sustain philosophical dialogue. Asked to form questions about a text, or to each other, students often responded by making declarative statements. At the beginning of the course many students could not even clearly distinguish assertions from questions. Influenced by an educational system that focuses mainly on "functionalism/production/training," and by religious and political institutions that nurture sets of dogmas and not forms of inquiry, some of the students in the class remarked that they were being asked and encouraged to form questions for the first time in their lives. In the beginning of the course, when, on rare occasions, students did create questions, the questions were typically of two types: questions that only demanded affirmation or negation (yes/no answers), or questions that sought to flush out details or immediately resolve doubts on a particular text. It was nearly five months into the course when students began to create questions that would provoke and maintain real challenges to their experience, questions that would "break open" their experience.[7] It was only then that we could say a philosophical relationship to questions and a deep experience of thinking was underway.

There is no methodology or formula that can be applied to teach someone how to ask philosophical questions, or that can be used to provoke someone to enter into a philosophical relationship with questions. Philosophy begins with wonder,[8] in both senses of the word—*awe* and *doubt*—because it is wonder that inspires us to ask and to ponder. In Caxias we simply tried to nurture wonder. But how does one nurture wonder? Wonder is nurtured by cultivating attention (*prosoche*), by allowing students to dwell in thinking. Attention, according to Hadot, is key to *spiritual exercise*.[9] It is continuous vigilance and presence of mind, a constant tension of the spirit (1995: 84). Attentive to the infinite value of each moment, we respond "immediately to events, as if they were questions asked of us all of a sudden" (ibid.: 85). We found that after months of attentively dwelling with paintings, music, conversation, and poetry shared by teachers, questions *had* to be asked. The call to thinking was too strong, the wonder too great. And so the students asked, and asked, and did not stop asking.

To live comfortably with uncertainty, mystery, and doubt, without irritable reaching after fact and reason, establishes what Susan Wolfson calls a "questioning presence" (1986). The English Romantic poet John Keats calls this disposition *negative capability* (Keats, 2001: 492), and it is this trait that distinguishes the great poets such as Shakespeare, Goethe, and Milton, and the great philosophers such as Socrates, Nietzsche, and Foucault from their colleagues. This questioning disposition is as fundamental to experiencing philosophy as it is to experiencing poetry, and the teachers and students in Caxias were asked from the first to the last moments of their philosophy course to nurture *negative capability*. A year-long experience of constant questioning rather than receiving answers, of living with doubts rather than certainties, of looking at reality as something mysterious rather than as something fixed and anesthetic, transformed the dispositions of the teacher and student participants in the project. It might explain why so many of our moments were poetic as much as they were philosophical.

9.6 Dialogue (being dialogued and being in dialogue)

During a moment of reflection on the course, Dona Andrezza, age fifty-four, shared with the class that she "felt empty after our encounters, philosophy was emptying me out." This was a striking observation that captures the profundity of the dialogues that occurred throughout the course. It also recalls many of Socrates' dialogues in which, rather than "fill" his interlocutors with knowledge, Socrates makes them question many of their beliefs and then discard them. This suggests that philosophical dialogue is often an experience of emptying ourselves out rather than filling ourselves up. Those who dialogue with Socrates do not learn something they did not know before; they learn that they do not know what they thought they knew. In a sense, like Dona Andrezza, they are "emptied."

Contemporary Brazilian poet Manoel de Barros expresses this nicely: "Unlearning eight hours a day teaches the principles [of] a didactics of invention" (2000: 9). In our teacher education courses this was a constant testimony of the teachers: the more they became engaged in philosophy the more clearly they could understand their journey with philosophy as an unlearning process. This experience of unlearning was complemented by, and related to, the *spiritual exercise* of "becoming a child," presented in de Barros' *Exercises of Being a child* (1999). Barros shows how we can learn from practicing a childish way of being in the world, in that children are accustomed to being less "full," "fresher," less prejudiced, and more open to freely put themselves into question. Engaged in this exercise of "being a child," students in Caxias were asked to try to do some activities—painting, drawing, making questions—as a child would do, as if they had never done these things before, as if they were doing them for the first time, as if anything were possible. Vinicius, age fifty-seven, captured the essence of this exercise nicely in one of our sessions when he told us that he was forming questions for the first time and that he felt as if he hadn't asked any questions in his life before.

This Socratic approach to the practice of philosophy has eminent pedagogical consequences. As Foucault stressed in his last course at the *Collège de France*, *Le courage de la vérité* (2009), devoted to the death of Socrates, the Athenian radically re-positioned the scope and sense of being a teacher. Where the traditional teacher said to the student: "You do not know and I know. Therefore, I will teach you so that you learn what you do not know." Socrates says: "You do not know, but I do not know either. So I will help you to take care of what you do not care about" (Foucault, 2009: 131–43). When Socrates' interlocutors think they know what they really do not know, Socrates' teaching consists in de-constructing this pseudo-knowledge. In his final *Apology* before the Athenian tribunal, Socrates deemed the judgment against him as a judgment against a philosophical life. He explained that his wisdom did not consist of any positive knowledge but of a singular relationship to knowledge that demanded he not delude himself regarding the impossibility of human beings having any certain knowledge. He reasoned that if, as the oracle had proclaimed, he were truly the wisest man in Athens, it was because he was the only one who did not believe he knew anything for certain, aside from his own lack of knowledge.

To be sure, the majority of the students, particularly at the beginning of the course, were expecting to be "filled" with information and beliefs. Accustomed to being told what to think and believe by their churches, political figures, bosses at work, teachers at school, and others, the process of participating in "emptying" rather than "filling" was at first painful and frustrating for many of the students. On more than one occasion students complained of "not learning anything," of having teachers that "don't teach." But dialogue as *spiritual exercise* "guides the interlocutor towards conversion" (Hadot, 1995: 93) and eventually our dialogues as "emptying" experiences began to provoke a transformation in the students of the course.

To put it in Socratic terms, this transformation has to do with that which we care for. This also implies a transformation of the function of the teacher. As Foucault (2009) pointed out in the case of Socrates, the teacher of philosophy occupies a paradoxical position in terms of care.

Socrates dialogued with everyone so that they would stop caring about the exterior—richness, fame, honors, and so on—and would be moved to care for what is interior—the soul, the truth, the good. One might interpret care for the self as an egocentric or individualistic movement, but Socrates' intention was quite the contrary. He wanted people to give importance to that which is most important in the individual and collective dimensions of life. In fact, Socrates materialized this project in his life: he was the only one who did not care about himself *ipsus litere* because he was continuously concerned with others caring about themselves. Yet, in another sense, he took care of himself in the deepest way possible: as a teacher, as a spiritual leader, as a philosopher—someone who helps others to take care of themselves.

Our communal experiences of dialogue in school led to another *spiritual exercise* concerning the care of self and others: meditation as dialogue with oneself. There is, argues Hadot, an "intimate connection between dialogue with others and dialogue with oneself. Only he who is capable of a genuine encounter with the other is capable of an authentic encounter with himself, and the converse is equally true" (1995: 91). Self-dialogue is not merely an encounter, but a confrontation with oneself. Hadot describes it as a "battle" amicable, but real. Though not eristic, every *spiritual exercise* is dialogical in this self-confrontational sense.

In Caxias we were able to see that dialogue with oneself and with others makes one unlearn what he has learned in a traditional way. Participants in our course came to question the relationship they had with knowledge, as something settled that they needed to receive. This kind of relationship had to be unlearned in order to build a new one: a questioning and dialogical relationship with knowledge. The same could be said in relation to thinking. What the students in Caxias had to learn was to unlearn a relationship with their own thinking as something they could not create or sustain themselves. Dialogue allowed the students to actively think about, and put into doubt the circumstances that made them live the way they were living. They began to think in new ways and created a new relationship with thinking. The significance of such an experience is apparent in another statement made by Vinicius, who told one of his teachers: "For the first time in my life I am pondering the stars, what is beyond, rather than being constantly weighed down by my everyday concerns of money, work, family problems, and health." Emptied and lighter, Vinicius, like Cynic and Stoic philosophers before him, was able to "take flight" and begin pondering the cosmos.

One of the most obvious impacts our project had on the adult participants is that it led them to see, think about, and be in the world in a different manner. The Stoics distinguished three branches of philosophy: *logic, physics, ethics*—each concerned with an aspect of one's being in the world. Typically, *spiritual exercises* are placed in *ethics*, but this is too limiting (Davidson in Hadot, 1995: 24). Hadot has demonstrated that within the Stoic tradition *logic* and *physics* were never merely areas of discourse, but were disciplines of the well-lived life (ibid.). Incidentally, this is one of Hadot's critiques of Foucault: that he claims that Foucault placed *spiritual exercises* firmly in the ethical realm, but didn't explore their place in realms of physics or logic (1995: 206–15 and Davidson in Hadot, 1995: 24). Hadot states that philosophical *physics* contains three levels of exercises:[10]

1 Contemplation as an end in itself. Serenity of soul, liberation from day to day worries.
2 A transcending of individuality to come into contact with the cosmos.
3 Contemplation of nature (the world) tears us away from everyday life. It makes us question received ideas. (1995: 103–4)

At each of these three levels it is possible to hear Vinicius talking! He could—for the first time—liberate himself from day-to-day worries (level 1), he could ponder the stars (level 2) and could tear himself away from, and question daily reality (level 3). Vinicius had fully engaged in the physical realm of *spiritual exercises*.

9.7 Political impacts of philosophy as a way of life in Duque de Caxias

Spiritual exercises are part of a philosophical way of living that provokes a radical transformation of being. We cannot say with certainty that the students and teachers who participated in the "Em Caxias a Filosofia En-caixa?!" project now live philosophically. But we can say that through philosophical exercises the majority of students and teachers involved in the project had a radical opportunity to transform themselves.

At the end of the course, when asked the question: "What does philosophy mean to you?" several students responded that philosophy had "taught them a lot." When pressed to expand on and clarify the response it became clear that the students lacked words to express their experiences with philosophy. Their experiences of sharing life experiences, of weaving oral texts, of questioning and dialoging as a group and individually, and of developing a doubting disposition that revealed a world full of mystery and intrigue, had produced individual and group experiences that were extremely intense and perhaps beyond words. These examples constitute proof that philosophy cannot merely be discussed, written, or read about; it must be lived and felt.

Though all impacts of the project in Caxias may not be immediately apparent, upon reflecting on the project it is evident that it had certain political effects. Before discussing these impacts a clarification is needed: our practice was not designed to produce any particular political outcome. We invited students to think, but we did not demand that they think in a certain way or toward certain ideas, much less that their thoughts correspond to our thoughts.

Two examples might help us express the political dimension of the project. During one class Luiza told a story about how, because of philosophy and our discussions in class, she felt more strength to question her husband and demand that he justify some of his demands on her. On another occasion, Valerio gave an emotional account of how he now felt more power to question his bosses and people on the street that didn't treat him respectfully. He also appealed to other students in the class to do the same, exclaiming that because of philosophy they should feel the self-confidence to "speak to power." Putting these statements into different words we might say that what these students came to realize was that they were more powerful than they had always been told, and that they might have more power over the way that they live, more power to live as they desire—if not in all aspects of their lives, at least in some of them.

Reading the work of Hadot one comes across a passage from G. Friedman's *La Puissance de la sagesse*:

> Take flight each day! At least for a moment, however brief, as long as it is intense. Every day a "spiritual exercise," alone or in the company of a man who also wishes to better himself...Leave ordinary time behind. Make an effort to rid yourself of your own passions...Become eternal by surpassing yourself. This inner effort is necessary, this ambition, just. *Many are those who are entirely absorbed in militant politics, in the preparation for the social revolution. Rare, very rare, are those who, in order to prepare for the revolution, wish to become worthy of it.* (Emphasis added.)[11]

Is our course in Caxias part of the preparation for social/political revolution? Does philosophy as we practice it have this role? Should it play this role? Is *spiritual exercise* in philosophy the preparation needed to bring about true social/political revolution? Though the political outcomes we documented in our project tended toward liberatory experiences, if we are really committed to self-questioning then we cannot settle these questions with one particular response. We must, rather, keep them alive as a way of constantly putting into question the meaning and sense of bringing philosophical *spiritual exercises* to public schools in Rio de Janeiro, Brazil.

Notes

Co-authored with Jason Thomas Wozniak, Member, Center of Philosophical Studies of Childhood (NEFI), State University of Rio de Janeiro (UERJ).

1 The original Português "Em Caxias a Filosofia En-caixa?!" plays with the word "Caxias" which is a city name but also signifies "fit."
2 Certainly the expression "spiritual exercises" is not free of misunderstanding, as P. Hadot (1995: 81–2) acknowledges. The word "spiritual' is full of metaphysical and theological connotations but the other expressions discussed, and ultimately rejected by Hadot, seem to present other problems: one might use the terms "thinking" or "intellectual" exercises, but both terms seem to leave aside a fundamental dimension of "spiritual exercises": imagination and sensibility. Another possible expression could be "ethical exercises" given that "spiritual exercises" contribute to a therapeutic of passions and refer to a conduct in life. But such an expression would be too limiting in that "spiritual exercises" imply a transformation of the world view and of the personality of the person practicing them.
3 For the complete lists see Hadot (1995: 84).
4 We owe this contribution to our colleague and friend Maximiliano Lopez.
5 Hadot places great emphasis on the fact that "Ancient philosophy itself is above all oral in character" (1995: 62). He states that Plato believed that "what is inscribed in the soul by the spoken word is more real and more lasting than letters drawn on papyrus or parchment" (ibid.). Ancient philosophy, "in the first instance seeks to form people and transform souls. That is why philosophical teaching is given above all in oral form, because only the living word, in dialogues, in conversations pursued for a long time, can accomplish such an action" (ibid.: 89–93). Philosophy in antiquity, "was thus essentially dialogue, a living relationship between people rather than an abstract relation to ideas" (Hadot 2009: 54).

6   An intriguing interview question from Arnold Davidson and response from Hadot shows a powerful way of relating philosophy to other artistic disciplines and also supports the use of artistic texts in the practice of philosophy:

> A.D.: "To see philosophy as a way of life and not only a coherent system of concepts and propositions has many consequences for the relationship between philosophy and the other literary and artistic disciplines. A novel, a poem, even a painting or music, can represent a way of life and sometimes provoke a transformation in our way of living. In this light, philosophy as a discipline does not insulate itself but opens itself to all the descriptions of our ways of living. Does this imply that we must rethink the borders of philosophy?"
>
> HADOT: "I would say that art can be a powerful auxiliary to philosophy, but it can never be life itself, the decision, the existential choice. The idea of a suppression of the limits between literature and philosophy was very much in style at the time of existentialism, but I believe it was already present in English or German Romanticism. Jean Wahl, for example, speaking of the relationship between poetry and metaphysics, defined romanticism as the rebirth of amazement; it makes familiar things strange, he said, and strange things familiar. He also added that art, for Bergson, was the power to lift the veil that habit weaves between us and things. This is why in a general way we can say that art, poetry, literature, painting, or even music can be a spiritual exercise" (Hadot 2009: 140).

7   For an insightful discussion on questions, cf. Hans-Georg Gadamer (2004).
8   Plato, *Theaetetus* 155d. Plato uses an infinitive as a noun: *to thaumazein* (to "be in wonder"), as a feeling (*pathos*) where philosophy finds its origin.
9   "Attention is a constant vigilance to the present moment" (Hadot 1995: 84). This means being present to the world, to ourselves, and to others in the world. When it is present to us, the present can also be called into question. Questioning and being attentive are two exercises that nurture each other. Questioning becomes a form of attentive presence in the world.
10 This discussion of *physics* by P. Hadot is also a central them in *The Veil of Isis* (2008), where Hadot presents philosophy not as a theoretical construct but as a method for training people to look at and live in the world in a new way.
11 One encounters this quote twice in Hadot (1995: 70, 81).

Appendices

Appendix A: Words of the EZLN in Juchitán

The afternoon is flickering out in the heat of the night. Shadows come down from the great Ceiba, the mother tree and sustenance of the world, picking any spot in which to put their mysteries to bed. Along with the afternoon, March is also going out, and not this one which surprises us today, going about with the many. I am speaking of another afternoon, in another time and in another land, ours. Old Antonio had returned from hoeing the field, and he sat down in the doorway of his hut. Inside, Dona Juanita was preparing tortillas and words. And, as she did so, she was passing them to Old Antonio, putting some in and taking others out, Old Antonio was muttering, while he smoked his rolled cigarette.

The history of the search

"Our most ancient wise men recount that the very first gods, those who birthed the world, had created almost all things, and they did not make everything, because they were aware that a goodly number should be created by men and women. That is why the gods who birthed the world, the most first, went away when the world was not yet complete. They did not go away without finishing it out of laziness, but because they knew that it was up to a few to begin, but finishing is the work of everyone. The most ancient of our most old also recount that the most first gods, those who birthed the world, had a knapsack where they had been keeping all the undone things they were leaving in their work. Not in order to do them later, but in order to have memory of what must come when men and women have finished the world which had been born incomplete.

And the gods who birthed the world, the most first, went away then. They left like the afternoon, as if putting themselves out, as if covering themselves in shadows, as if they were not there even though they were there. Then the rabbit, who was angry with the gods because they had not made him big even though he had carried out the tasks they had assigned him (monkeys, tigers, lizards), went and nibbled at the gods' knapsack, but he was noisy and the gods noticed and they pursued him in order to punish him for the crime he had committed. The rabbit ran quickly. That is why rabbits do indeed eat as if they had committed a crime and run away quickly if anyone sees them. The fact is that, even though he was unable to entirely rip open the knapsack of the most first gods, the rabbit always does manage to make a hole. Then, when the gods who had birthed the world went away, all the undone things fell out of the hole in the knapsack. And the most first gods did not even realize it, and then one came whom they called wind and it took to blowing and blowing, and the undone things went in one direction and the other, and, since it was night, no one knew where they had gone so they could stop those undone things which were the things which had to be created in order for the world to be complete.

When the gods became aware of the mess, they made a huge racket and they became very sad and they say that some even wept. That is why they say that, when it is going to rain, first the sky makes much noise and then the water comes. The men and women of maize, the true ones, heard the bawling, because when the gods cry it can indeed be heard far away. The men and women of maize then went to see why the most first gods were crying, those who birthed the world, and then, between sobs, the gods recounted to them what had happened. And then the men and women of maize said: "Do not cry anymore. We are going to look for the undone things which were lost, because we already know that there are things undone, and that the world will not be complete until everything is made and fixed up." And the men and women of maize went on to say: "Then let us ask you, most first gods, those who birthed the world, whether you remember a bit of the undone things which were lost, so that we may then know if what we find are undone things, or if they are something new which are already being birthed."

The most first gods did not reply then, because their bawling was preventing them even from speaking. And then, later, while they were rubbing their eyes in order to clean away their tears, they said: "An undone thing is each person finding themselves."

That is why our most ancient say that when we are born, we are born lost, and then, as we grow up, we go about seeking ourselves, and that living is seeking, looking for ourselves.

And, more calmed down now, the gods who birthed the world, the most first, went on to say: "All those things yet to be born in the world have to do with this, which we are telling you, with each person finding himself. That is how you will know if what you find is something yet to be born in the world, if it helps you find yourselves."

"That is good," said the true men and women, and they set about seeking everywhere the undone things which must be created in the world and which would help them find themselves.

Old Antonio finished the tortillas, the cigarette and the words. He remained still for a while, looking at a corner of the night. After a few minutes, he said: "Since then, we go about seeking, seeking ourselves. We seek when we are working, when we are resting, when we are eating and when we are sleeping, when we are loving and when we are dreaming. When we live seeking ourselves and seeking ourselves seeking when we have already died. In order to find ourselves we seek ourselves, in order to find ourselves we live and we die."

"And how does one go about finding oneself?" I asked.

Old Antonio kept looking at me, and he said to me, while rolling another cigarette: "An old wise Zapotec told me how. I am going to tell you, but in Spanish, because only those who have found themselves can speak the Zapoteca tongue well, which is the flower of the word, and my word is barely seed, and there are others which are stem and leaves and fruit, and the one who is complete finds that. The father Zapotec said:

First you shall walk all the paths of all the peoples of the earth, before finding yourself. [Niru zazalu' guira'xixe neza guidxilayu' ti ganda guidxelu' lii]"

I took note of what Old Antonio told me that afternoon in which March and the afternoon were putting themselves out. Since then, I have walked many paths, but not all, and I am still seeking the face which will be seed, stem, leaf, flower and fruit of the word. I seek myself with everything and in everything in order to be complete.

A light was smiling in the night above, as if she would find herself in the shadow below.
March is going. But hope is arriving."
Subcomandante Insurgente Marcos.
Juchitán, Oaxaca.

Mexico,
March 31, 2001

Appendix B

Here are some of our shared action principles or "gestures" available to teachers in our Project (see www.filoeduc.org/caxias). Their inspiration is multiple and they are constantly changing from the outcomes of our practice:

Gestures of affirmation

What is, in our perspective, important that the teacher do in her practice?

1. Encourage the participants to listen and to dialogue with each other. Highlight the similarities and the differences between the perspectives presented. Ask for clarification when what was said seems confused. Seek to deepen each perspective, and encourage participants to do the same.
2. Ask "why, and persist in asking." Insist on consistency. Problematize the sense of what is happening.
3. Help participants to explore each question in depth. Do not bombard them with questions, but explore each of them.
4. Don't be bothered by silence. Try to observe different forms of attention. Participation is not always in spoken form.
5. Discourage long monologues so that voice is shared within the group; orchestrate scattered ideas, stitching them together as a collective dialogue.
6. Do not impose anything that the group does not need. For example, if the group requires rules, they must produce them themselves.

Gestures to avoid

What practices inhibit, in our consideration, the potential of philosophical thinking?

1. Lecturing.
2. Attempting to control, discipline, or evaluate what a student knows.
3. Answering a question in a way that ignores or occludes doubt.
4. Voicing moral judgments about students' thoughts and affirmations.
5. Talking too much. Open questions, briefly put, are preferable. Contributing an anecdotal or opinionated conversation in like manner.
6. Seeking to solve personal problems, although the conversation often helps to think through those problems.

Ways of thinking together about our work

What dispositions contribute to the work we are fostering to unfold?

A. Dispositions concerning the questions and topics investigated
   1. Is our thinking stimulated by our inquiry?
   2. Do we wonder, express curiosity, and become deeply involved in the discussion?
   3. Do we think the same way as we did before the inquiry, or have we changed our position?
   4. Do fresh questions arise? Are some of our questions transformed by the inquiry?

B. Dispositions regarding the participants
   1. Do we help to build an atmosphere of trust, in which everyone felt that their thinking would be heard carefully?
   2. Do we encourage the participants to express their views when they seem doubtful about joining in?
   3. Do we try to involve as many participants, in as many different ways, as possible?
   4. Do we promote dialogue between participants, rather than between participants and teacher?

5. Do we foster cooperation in the inquiry?
6. Do we take the views of the participants into consideration, giving each the opportunity to be heard, understood, and responded to?
7. Are we sensitive to the length of each intervention?
8. Do we avoid manipulating the inquiry to impose a point of view?
9. Do we help students to relate their ideas with their experience and with other knowledge?

C. Dispositions regarding the inquiry
1. Do we seek to bring the dialogue to a deeper conceptual level through problematizing assumptions or implicit values?
2. Do we try to focus the discussion when it becomes too abstract or unclear?
3. Do we take care to explore the inquiry's direction, implications, and assumptions, in a search for underlying reasons and not an exchange of opinions?
4. Do we help to avoid the idea that philosophical investigations serve only to confirm predetermined answers?
5. Do we trust and help others to trust that there may be growth in philosophical inquires?
6. Do we help participants to clarify and develop what they say?
7. Do we help to connect and relate the ideas of the participants through suggesting, for example, lines of convergence or divergence?
8. Do we encourage participants to explore positions that they do not agree with?
9. Do we point out possible contradictions, and in other cases, consistencies?
10. Do we indicate possible ways of continuing of the inquiry?

Bibliography

Agamben, G. (2000/1978). Enfance et historie [Childhood and History]. Paris: Payot & Rivages.

Arendt, H. (1959) "Reflections on Little Rock." In *Dissent*, v. 6, n. 1, pp. 45–55.

———. (1961) "The Crises of Education." In Arendt. *Between Past and Future: Six Exercises in Political Thought*. New York: The Viking Press, pp. 173–96.

Ariès, Ph. (1973 [1960]), *L'Enfant et la vie familiale sous l'ancient regime*. Paris: Seuil (2nd edn) and Librairie Plon (1st edn).

Aristotle (2003). *Physics*. Engl. Transl. R. P. Hardie & R. K. Gaye. Adelaide: The University of Adelaide Press.

Ball, S. (ed., 1990). *Foucault and Education: Disciplines and Knowledge*. New York: Routledge.

Barros, M. de. (1999). *Exercícios de ser Criança*. Rio de Janeiro: Salamandra.

———. (2000) *O livro das ignorâças*. São Paulo: Record.

———. (2010). *Memórias inventadas. As infâncias de Manoel de Barros*. São Paulo: Planeta.

Baudrillard, J. (2002). "The Dark Continent of Childhood." In Baudrillard. *Screened Out*. Engl. Transl. Chris Turner. London: Verso, pp. 102–6.

Bergson, H. (1946). *The Creative Mind: An Introduction to Metaphysics*. Engl. Transl. Mabelle L. Anderson. New York: Dover Publications.

Bernstein, B. (1990). *The Structuring of Pedagogical Discourse: Class, Codes and Control*. Vol. IV. London: Routledge.

Berríos, M. & Kohan, W. (1995). *Una otra mirada: niñas y niños pensando en América Latina*. Puebla: Universidad Iberoamericana.

Borges, J. L. (1974). *Obras Completas*. Buenos Aires: Emecé.
Deleuze, G. (1990). *Pourparlers*. Paris: Les Éditions de Minuit.
——. (1995). *Logique du sens*. Paris: Les Éditions de Minuit.
——. (2003). *Différence et Répétition*. Paris: Presses Universitaires de France. [*Difference and Repetition*. Engl. Transl. Paul Potton. London: The Athlone Press, 1997].
——. (2004). *Proust et les signes*. Paris: Presses Universitaires de France.
Deleuze, G. & Guattari, F. (1980). *Capitalisme et Schizophrenie tome 2: Mille plateaux*. Paris: Les Éditions de Minuit.
——. (1991). *Qu'est-ce que la philosophie?* Paris: Les Éditions de Minuit. [*What Is Philosophy?* Engl. Trans. Graham Burchell and Hugh Tomlinson. New York: Columbia University Press].
Derrida, J. (1980). *La carte postale*. Paris: Flammarion.
——. (1990). *Du Droit à la Philosophie*. Paris: Gallimard.
——. (1997). *De l'hospitalité. Anne Dufourmantelle invite Jacques Derrida à répondre*. Paris: Calmann-Lévy.
EZLN (1996). *Documentos y comunicados*. México: ERA.
Ferraro, G. (1990). *I giardini di Armida o della solitudine del filosofo*. Napoli: Athena.
——. (2010a). *Filosofia fueri le mura*. Napoli: Filema.
——. (2010b). *La scuola dei sentimenti*. Napoli: Filema.
Foucault, M. (1977). "Preface." In Deleuze, Gilles & Guattari, Félix. *Anti-Oedipus: Capitalism and Schizophrenia*. New York: Viking Pres, pp. xi–xiv.
——. (1983). "The Subject and the Power." In Dreyfus, H. & Rabinow, P., *Michel Foucault. Beyond Structuralism and Hermeneutics: Afterword* (2nd edn). Chicago: The University of Chicago Press, pp. 208–26.
——. (1984). *Histoire de la sexualité*. Paris: Gallimard, t. II: *L'usage des plaisirs*. [*The Usage of Pleasures*. Engl. Transl. Robert Hurley. New York: Vintage Books, 1996]
——. (1994a). *Dits et Écrits. 1954–1988*. Vol. II (1970–1975). Paris: Gallimard.
——. (1994b). *Dits et Écrits. 1954–1988*. Vol. IV (1980–1988). Paris: Gallimard.
——. (1997). *Surveiller et punir. Naissance de la prison*. Paris: Gallimard.
——. (2001). *L'herméneutique du sujet*. Paris : Gallimard-Seuil. [*The Hermeneutics of the Subject*: Lectures at the College de France, 1981–1982. Engl. Transl Graham Burchell, ed. Frederic Gros. New York: Palgrave Macmillan].

———. (2009). *Le courage de la vérité*. Paris: Gallimard.
Freire, P. (1992). *A Importância do Ato de Ler*. São Paulo: Cortez.
Gadamer, H.-G. (1999). *Verdade e Método*. Petrópolis: Vozes, p. 512.
Gadamer, H.-G. (2004). *Truth and Method*. Engl Transl. Joel Weinsheimer & Donald G. Marshall. London: Continuum.
Gaos, J. (1947). *Filosofía de la filosofía e historia de la filosofía*. México: Stylo.
Goering, S., Shudak, N. J. & Wartenberg, Th. E. (eds., 2013). *Philosophy in Schools*. New York: Routledge.
Hadot, P. (1993). *Exercices spirituels et philosophie antique*. Paris: Albin Michel.
———. (1995). *Philosophy as a Way of Life: Spiritual Exercises from Socrates to Foucault*. Engl Transl. Michael Chase. Oxford: Blackwell Publishing.
———. (2002). *What Is Ancient Philosophy?* Engl Transl. Michael Chase. Cambridge: Belknap Press of Harvard University Press.
———. (2006). *The Veil of Isis: An Essay on the History of the Idea of Nature*. Engl Transl. Michael Chase. Cambridge: Belknap Press of Harvard University Press.
———. (2009). *The Present Alone Is Our Happiness: Conversations with Jeannie Carlier & Arnold I. Davidson*. Engl. Transl. Marc Djaballah. Stanford: Stanford University Press.
Heraclitus (2001). *Maior Edition by Miroslav Marcovich*. Sankt Augustin: Academia Verlag.
Jaspers, K. (1959). "Way to Wisdom." In Jaspers. *Introduction to Philosophy*. Engl. Transl. Ralph Manheim. New Haven: Yale University Press.
Kant, I. (1929). *Critique of Pure Reason*. Engl. Transl. Norman Kemp Smith. London: MacMillan.
Keats, J. (2001). *Complete Poems and Selected Letters of John Keats*. New York: The Modern Library.
Kennedy, D. (2006a). *The Well of Being: Childhood, Subjectivity, and Education*. Albany: SUNY Press.
———. (2006b). *Changing Conceptions of the Child from the Renaissance to Post-Modernity: A Philosophy of Childhood*. Lewiston, NY: The Mellen Press.
———. (2010). "Ann Sharp's Contribution: A Conversation with Matthew Lipman." *Childhood & Philosophy*, vol. 6, n. 11, 11–19.
———. (2011). *Philosophical Dialogue with Children: Essays on Theory and Practice*. Lewiston, NY: The Mellen Press.

Kitchener, R. F. (1990). "Do Children Think Philosophically?" *Metaphilosophy*, vol. 21, n. 4, 416–31.

Kohan, W. O. (2001). "Some questions to/within *Philosophy for Children.*" *Ethik und Sozialwissenschaften*, vol. 4, n. 12, 443–6.

——. (2003). *Infância. Entre educação e filosofia*. Belo Horizonte, MG: Autêntica, 2003.

Kohan, W. O. & Olarieta, F. (eds., 2012). *A escola pública aposta no pensamento*. Belo Horizonte: Autêntica.

Kohan, W. O. & Waksman, V. (1997). *¿Qué es filosofía para niños? Ideas y propuestas para pensar la educación*. Buenos Aires: La UBA y los Profesores/Oficina de Publicaciones CBC (Universidad de Buenos Aires).

——. (2000). *Filosofía con niños. Aportes para el trabajo en clase*. Buenos Aires: Novedades Educativas.

Kohan, W. O. Leal, B., Teixiera, A. (eds., 2000). *Filosofia na Escola Pública*. Petrópolis, RJ: Vozes.

Larrosa, J. (1996) *La experiencia de la lectura*. Barcelona: Laertes.

——. (2000). *Pedagogía Profana*. Buenos Aires: Novedades Educativas.

Liddell, H. & Scott, R. (1966). *A Greek English Lexicon*. Oxford: Clarendon Press.

Lipman, M. (1967) *Harry Stottlemier's Discovery*. Upper Montclair: IAPC.

——. (1988). *Philosophy Goes to School*. Philadelphia: Temple University Press.

——. (1990). "Response to Professor Kitchener (1990)." *Metaphilosophy*, vol. 24, n. 4, 432–3.

——. (1991). *Thinking in Education* (1st edn). Cambridge: University Press.

——. (ed., 1993). *Thinking Children and Education*. Dubuque, Iowa: Kendall.

——. (1998). "The Contributions of Philosophy to Deliberative Democracy." In Evans, David, Kuçuradi, Ioanna (eds.). *Teaching Philosophy on the Eve of the Twenty-First Century*. Ankara, Turkey: International Federation of Philosophical Societies, pp. 6–29.

——. (2001). "Philosophy for Children: Some Assumptions and Implications" & "Answers to My Critics." *Ethik und Sozialwissenschaften*, vol. 4, n. 12, 405–17 & 465–80.

——. (2003). *Thinking in Education* (2nd edn). Cambridge: Cambridge University Press.

——. (2008). *A Life Teaching Thinking: An Autobiography*. Upper Montclair: IAPC.

Lipman, M., Sharp, A. M. & Oscanyan, F. S. (1980) *Philosophy in the Classroom*. Temple: Temple University Press.

Masschelein, J. (1990). "L'éducation comme action. A propos de la pluralité et de la naissance." *Orientamenti Pedagogici*, vol. xxxvii, n. 4, 760–71.

Matthews, G. (1994). *The Philosophy of Childhood*. Cambridge, Mass.: Harvard University Press.

Nefi. (2011). *Caderno de materiais*. Rio de Janeiro: UERJ.

Neruda, P. (1974). *Confieso que he vivido*. Barcelona: Seix Barral.

Nietzsche, F. (2003) *The Genealogy of Morals*. New York: Dover.

Ong, W. J. (2002). Orality and Literacy. New York: Routledge.

Plato (1989). *The Collected Dialogues,* ed., Edith Hamilton and Hungtington Cairns. Princeton: Princeton University Press, Bollingen Series LXXII.

——. (1990). *Platonis Opera*, ed. John Burnet. Oxford: Oxford University Press.

Postman, N. (1982). *The Disappearance of Childhood*. New York: Delacorte Press.

Rancière, J. (1987). *Le maître ignorant*. Paris: Fayard [*The Ignorant Schoolmaster*. Engl. Transl. Kristin Ross. Stanford: Stanford University Press, 1991].

——. (1995). *La mésentente. Politique et Philosophie*. Paris: Galilée.

Rodríguez, S. (2001a). *Cartas*. Caracas: Ediciones del Rectorado de la UNISER.

——. (2001b). *Obra Completa*. Tomo I. Caracas: Presidencia de la República.

——. (2001c). *Obra Completa*. Tomo II. Caracas: Presidencia de la República.

Sharp, A. (ed., 1994). "Women, Feminism and Philosophy for Children." *Thinking: The Journal of Philosophy for Children*. Special double issue, vol. XI, n. 3–4.

Wolfson, S. J. (1986). *The Questioning Presence: Wordsworth, Keats, and the Interrogative Mode in Romantic Poetry*. Ithaca: Cornell University Press.

Index

abilities 40, 47, 49, 54, 59, 64, 86, 89–91, 98, 103
academy 14, 25
adults 3, 14, 16, 18–19, 33, 35, 50, 55, 56–9, 64–5, 76, 87–8, 90, 97–8, 100, 102–3, 111
aesthetics 6, 63, 95
Agamben, Giorgio 18
age 24, 27, 40, 55, 64, 76, 88, 99
aion, *see* time
aporia x, 41
Arendt, Hannah 23–4, 34, 36
Aristotle 7, 15–17, 63, 70, 90, 102
askesis 100–1
assumptions 4, 6, 10, 13, 16, 29, 31, 37, 39, 54–6, 65, 78, 89, 120
Athenians, the 16, 32, 36, 41, 90, 98, 109
attention 4, 6, 70, 74, 85–6, 91, 101, 107, 114, 118
attitudes 30, 32, 38, 47, 55, 76

Barros, Manoel de 11, 15–16, 95, 96, 108
becoming ix, 17, 24, 92, 95, 108
beginning 15, 18, 20, 36, 66–7, 69–70, 72–3, 85
body 7, 26, 32, 82–3
Bolívar, Simón 90, 96
Borges, Jorge Luis 17
Brasília 3, 44–5, 60, 72

capability, negative viii, x, 108

capacity x, 6, 15, 18, 24, 47, 71, 78, 91
capitalism 31, 84
care 32, 45, 53–4, 64, 66, 71, 101, 105, 109–10, 120
Caxias, Duque de 3, 87–8, 98–9, 102–8, 110–13, 118
childhood
  relation to philosophy (and education) ix–xiii, 22, 26–7, 31, 41–2, 64–7
  what is? viii, xii, 12–20, 40, 49, 55, 59, 64–6, 71–4, 85–6, 92, 95
children, voice of 55–60, 62–74, 76–83
chronos *see* time
citizenship 19, 33–7, 64, 75, 83–4
community of inquiry 5, 10, 12, 94
concepts 6–7, 16, 20, 31, 35–6
consequences 51–2, 54, 100, 109, 114
contradictions 15, 120
cooperation 47–8, 51–4, 64–5, 120
courage (of truth) 55, 109
creation/creativity 5, 18, 26, 35, 64, 66, 70, 77–8, 83, 87, 91, 95, 102, 104–5
critique ix, 3–4, 9, 28, 36–7, 111
curiosity 51, 119
curriculum 14, 24–6, 45, 89

Cynics 110

Davidson, Arnold 111, 114
death 22, 25, 29, 39, 41, 79–81, 109
Deleuze, Gilles 17–18, 28, 31, 37–8, 91–2, 96, 102
deliberation 9, 35
democracy ix, 8–10, 19–20, 23, 29, 35, 41, 53, 64–5, 83–4
Derrida, Jacques 91–2
Descartes 78
development 14, 19, 32–3, 47, 56, 84–5
Dewey, John 5, 8, 23–5
dialogue 13, 32, 35, 42, 62, 69, 76, 80, 82, 84, 86, 97–8, 102–6, 108–10, 113, 118–20
didactics 5, 8, 108
difference 12, 19, 35, 38–41
discipline 4–6, 10, 26, 29, 45, 48, 69, 74, 85, 101, 111, 114, 119
discussion 10, 54, 56–60, 62, 77, 82, 95, 102, 104–5, 112, 114
dispositions 33–4, 47, 48, 52, 54, 86, 90, 102, 107–8, 112, 119–20
dissatisfaction 7, 50–1
dogmatism 85
dominant 16, 19–20, 40, 47, 50, 52, 56, 64, 68, 74, 89–90, 92
drawing 62, 79, 103, 108

encounter 38–42, 48, 66, 76, 93, 105, 110
ends 50, 54
enigma viii, 73
epistemology 14, 17, 98, 101, 103
equality 91, 95
ethics 10, 14, 17, 23, 52, 70, 90, 111, 113
evaluation 49, 92
exclusion 10, 41, 50, 66, 93–4
experience
    as such 17–19, 91
    hermeneutical sense 37–9
    human 104, 106–7, 112
    of birth/childhood 36, 74, 84–5
    of thinking 4–5, 8–9, 13, 24, 31, 37, 40–2, 49, 60, 74, 76, 88–95, 98–101, 104, 112

fascism 20
Ferraro, Giuseppe 92, 93, 105
foreigner 67–9
formation
    education as formation 8, 31–4, 37, 40, 42, 64–6, 86
    formation of childhood 33, 64, 72, 83, 85
    teacher formation 25, 45, 88, 90, 93, 98, 108
Foucault, Michel 10, 20, 29–30, 50, 63, 74, 91–2, 96, 101, 105, 107, 109, 111
freedom 35, 57, 65, 74, 90
Freire, Paulo 25, 98, 103–4
friendship 61, 69–70, 92

gender 40, 59
Greeks, the 7, 16

Hadot, Pierre 97–8, 100, 102, 106–7, 109, 110–4
Hegel 78
Heraclitus 17–18, 42, 63, 75, 79–80, 83
history 5, 7, 14, 17–19, 35–6, 45, 48, 50, 69, 74, 84, 98, 100, 115
human rights 10

ideal 5, 10, 14, 31, 33, 64
ideas, philosophical 4, 7, 9–10, 33, 38, 40, 60, 94, 111, 120
ideology 10
ignorance 87, 89
imagination 38, 53, 113
imitation 39, 90
implications 4, 51–2, 54–5, 104, 120
impossible 4, 38, 41, 65, 104
Institute for the Advancement of Philosophy for Children (IAPC) 3, 12–4, 19
institution 3–4, 9–10, 22–3, 29–30, 42
intelligence 83, 91
interpretations 54, 62–4, 69, 103, 105, 110
intimacy 16, 20, 95–6
invention ix, 15, 32, 71, 81–2, 90, 95–6, 108

Jacotot, Joseph 91, 96
judgment 19, 35, 63, 80–1, 109, 119

Kant, Immanuel 4, 78
Keats, John 107
Kennedy, David 22, 86
knowledge 6, 29, 34–9, 47, 50, 53–4, 69–70, 88–93, 101, 103–4, 106, 108–110

language 13, 18–19, 24, 26, 67, 71, 90
Latin America 3, 7, 10, 29, 48, 74, 78, 87, 90
learning 4, 38–40, 47, 53, 67–8, 71–2, 76, 85, 89–94, 100, 104–5, 108–9
Leibniz 63
liberation 41–2, 77, 111, 113
life 6, 16–17, 20, 32, 36, 50–1, 73–4, 79–82, 89–90, 93–5, 100–1, 104, 109–11
Lipman, Matthew 2–10, 12, 14–15, 21–7, 35, 45, 48, 93–4
Literacy 88, 97–9, 103, 105
Logic 5, 9–10, 15, 17, 24, 31, 35, 54, 65, 68, 84, 90, 111
love 3, 16, 29–30, 34, 39, 51, 117

manuals 8, 14, 25–6
Marcos, Subcommandant 94–5
market 10, 84
mathematics 10, 75, 84
meaning x, 6–7, 9, 14–15, 26, 31, 33, 50, 62–3, 72, 77–8, 80, 83, 85, 90, 94, 105, 113
means (as opposed to ends) 9, 13, 50, 105
memories 12, 15, 20, 22
Mendham 12–4, 25–6
method ix, 3–4, 13–4, 26, 44, 47–9, 93, 95, 101–2, 107
model 3, 8–10, 24, 33
morals 30–1, 33, 37, 41, 85, 101, 109
natures 7, 16, 19, 33–4, 38, 50–1, 58, 81–2, 85, 100, 102, 111

NEFI 88, 96, 99, 113
Nietzsche 10, 30, 63, 83, 107

normal 37–8, 50, 54, 66–7, 90–1
novels 8, 10, 14, 25–6, 114
novelty 33, 36

openness 86, 89
opinion 57, 119–20
oppression 50, 59, 94
optimism 29–30
other, the 20, 30, 34, 39, 53, 66–7, 70–4, 78, 91, 100

paradox 4, 92, 109
pedagogy 4, 19, 34, 36, 42, 46–8, 52–4, 56, 64, 66–8, 76, 88–90, 109
perspective 1–2, 11, 16, 26, 29–31, 40, 65, 93
Philo of Alexandria 101
philosopher 4, 25, 33–5, 37, 63, 85, 92, 100, 110
philosophy
  at Public Schools 44–60, 87–96
  Philosophy for Children ix, 3–10, 12, 22, 25–6, 29, 45–7, 72, 83–4, 93
  philosophy with children 3, 32, 44, 48–9, 61, 64–6, 72–87
  what is? viii, 5–10, 37–42, 100–2
Plato 8–9, 16–18, 24, 28, 31–6, 41–2
Plato's Dialogues 42, 84, 106
  Apology 80, 96, 98, 106, 109
  Gorgias 41, 84
  Letter VII 106
  Phaedrus 104
  Republic 8, 24, 31–6, 42, 84
  Statesman 106
  Theaetetus 114
  Timeus 16–17
play xi, 17, 55–9, 80
politics 8–9, 32–6, 41–2, 66–7, 84, 90, 94–5
power 17, 41, 50–1, 56, 59, 70–1, 76, 90, 104, 112
pragmatism 4, 22, 25
problem posing/solving 6, 47, 60
problematization x, 5–8, 47, 52–5, 59–60, 66, 78, 84, 88–9, 102–6, 118, 120

questioning ix–x, 5–9, 42, 49–53, 70–1, 89, 93, 101–8, 112–14

race 40
Rancière, Jacques 91, 96
reading 14, 20, 2–4, 26, 31, 46, 62–4, 70, 77–80, 83, 95, 98, 101, 103–5, 112
reason 4, 8, 24, 54, 61–4, 74, 90, 109, 120
rebellion 17, 74, 94
recognition 15, 37, 38
research 23, 47, 55, 88
resistance ix, 42, 50, 53, 94
revolution 4, 9, 31, 74, 112–13
Rio de Janeiro 3, 46, 87–8, 98–9, 103
Rodríguez, Simón 90, 95–6

same, the 37–40, 73
School
 as institution 4, 10, 19, 22, 25–6, 29, 35, 42, 46, 57, 64, 68, 70, 74, 83
 elementary school 26, 29, 45, 46, 49, 60
 high school 29, 45, 46
 public school 44–52, 55, 60, 87–8, 97–9, 113
search 15, 48, 51, 53, 63, 73, 77–9, 88–9, 92, 95, 115, 120
Sharp, Ann Margaret 3, 14, 21, 22, 23, 25, 93, 94
Socrates 6, 10, 28, 32, 34, 41–2, 80, 82, 84, 86, 89–90, 96, 98, 102, 104–10
Solidarity 52–3, 65
Spinoza 23
spiritual exercises 97, 100–14
Stoics, The 110–11
strength 4, 78, 83, 93, 95
style 12, 14
subjectivity 6, 12, 50–1, 59, 92, 104
subversion 36, 41

teaching 37–41, 47, 53, 67, 72, 88, 92, 100, 102, 109, 113

thinking ix–xi, 15–16, 20, 31, 35, 37–41, 67–74, 76–80, 83, 84–5, 89–96, 104–17, 110
 critical 4–5, 8, 26, 30, 35, 48, 52–3, 64, 98, 103–4
 dogmatic image of 31, 37–8, 40
 philosophical 4, 6, 8–9, 13, 37–41
time 56–9, 85, 109–12
 as *aion* xii, 11, 16–20
 as *chronos* xii, 11, 16–17
 as *kairos* xii, 11, 16
tolerance 8, 9, 35, 64
toys 27, 58, 59
transformation ix, 9, 12–13, 19, 30, 65, 74, 83, 90, 93, 101–2, 109, 111, 113–14
travel 12–13, 22, 48, 52, 94, 106
truth 5, 15, 41, 51, 64, 69, 90, 95, 110

understanding 38, 52, 54–5, 57, 63, 65, 68–9, 71, 78, 85, 89
unexpectable 42
uniqueness 18, 27, 30, 37, 87
United States 22–3, 25, 30, 45
unlearn x, 94–6, 108, 110
unthinkable 15, 29, 40, 41, 63
utopia 8–9, 33, 35, 42

values 6, 9, 13, 21, 32, 47–8, 51–7, 65, 85, 90, 120
voice 36, 41, 53, 59, 66, 71, 76, 93–4, 105, 118

walk 78, 90, 117
wonder 9, 50–1, 107, 114, 119
words 7, 12, 16–17, 52, 62, 64, 67, 69, 71–2, 78, 85, 89, 93–4, 103–4, 113, 115, 117
world ix, 6, 9, 16–19, 36–7, 50–4, 60, 65–6, 70, 89–90, 95–6, 98, 103–14
writing 5, 22, 24, 26, 64, 95–6, 104

Zapatists, the 77–8, 94–6

Printed in the USA
CPSIA information can be obtained
at www.ICGtesting.com
LVHW091829261123
764947LV00004B/82